David O. Oyedepo

COMMANDING THE SUPERNATURAL

COMMANDING THE SUPERNATURAL

ISBN 978-978-2905-44-4

Reprint 2007, 2019, 2020, 2023, 2024

Published in Nigeria by:

DOMINION PUBLISHING HOUSE

For further information or permission, address:

Km 10, Idiroko Road, Canaan Land, Ota, Nigeria.

Tel: +234 816 406 0777, +234 909 151 4022

Or visit our website: ***www.dphprints.com***

Connect with David O. Oyedepo

@davidoyedepomin *davidoyedepomin*

faithtabernacle.org.ng *David Oyedepo Ministries International*

All Scripture quotations are from the King James Version of th Bible, except otherwise stated.

Contents

Introduction

They know not, neither will they understand; they walk on in darkness: all the foundations of the earth are out of course.

I have said, Ye are gods; and all of you are children of the most High.

But ye shall die like men, and fall like one of the princes.

Psalm 82:5-7

Whatever God has said is not subject to any opposition on the earth – the fierceness of the devil notwithstanding. But there is a key to dominion; there is a key for unlocking the forces that put you permanently in charge. Knowledge is the key. It turns frustration into fulfilment, sweat into sweetness, trials into testimonies and obstacles into miracles. Nothing can begin to match the power of knowledge.

Knowledge is the only guarantee for entering into your inheritance. God has placed within each one of us enough current that would give us light and make life meaningful and fulfilling. But due to ignorance, many are still grovelling in poverty, disease and all kinds of oppressive hardship of the enemy.

Therefore, may I submit that whatever is not working in your life is not God's fault! It is your knowledge that is inadequate. You need your own license of knowledge to walk in total freedom on this earth. For instance, think about this, the Word of God makes it clear that you are divine in nature, created after the very image of God. In fact, God said in Genesis 1:26:

> ***Let us make man in our image, after our likeness.***

He further reaffirms that you are in His class of being in Psalm 82:6:

> ***I have said, Ye are gods; and all of you are children of the most High.***

However, like the Jews of old, many believers, either out of ignorance or religion, think it is blasphemous to place man in the class of God. No wonder they have lost control or dominion over the affairs of life. The natural rules them. Darkness dogs their every path.

One of the greatest discoveries you can make about yourself is to know you are a spirit after the order of God. You are not designed to be subjected to the same limitations as other mortal men. In God's agenda, you are not programmed to die like men and fall like one of the princes. But until the truth of your divinity dawns on you, and you walk in it, you cannot be in control; you cannot command the supernatural, and you cannot operate like the son of whom you are.

Friend, only ignorance of your true nature will prevent your distinction. Understanding your divine nature (that you are in the class of God) is the key to commanding the supernatural. This will give you the confidence you need to operate like God in the affairs of life. But for it to produce, you must know it, understand it and walk in the light of it.

The knowledge of the supernatural is very relevant to a life of triumph and fulfilment. Without such knowledge, anyone will lose control of the affairs of life. This is because every natural happening is determined by the supernatural. Therefore, the supernatural is the foundation of all things, and just as the foundation of any natural building, the reality of the supernatural may not easily be comprehended, yet, it is the control room of all things – the natural answers to it.

For instance, the Bible reveals that Job was confronted with a catalogue of woes, so he concluded that God was behind his misfortunes. But the Bible is full of evidence of the reality of an evil spirit realm under the control of Satan, a realm from where he manipulates the destinies of his victims and inflicts evil on those under his control. Apostle John brings us to an awareness of this fact in 1 John 5:19:

> ***And we know that we are of God, and the whole world lieth in wickedness.***

Of course, that excludes you because...*we know that we are of God*. If God is your Father, the events happening in your life will be nothing less than what is happening in Heaven!

Every born-again believer is a child of God, and because God is a spirit, you belong to the class of the spirits. What you see of your physical self is not the real you; it is only a covering. The real you is spirit. By the law of life, like can only beget like. A goat only gives birth to a goat, a lion, a lion and so forth. From today you will manifest the reality of your divine status.

This book has been repackaged to provoke you to rise and take charge of the events of your life! As you rediscover your roots in God, you will begin to unlock the vast potential of the supernatural for your welfare in life.

From now on, you will begin to reign in life! You will break free from the shackles of poverty, disease, defeat and all the negative forces that keep men from fulfilling the purpose of God for their lives! Welcome to the unmolestable, unchallengeable, undefeatable realm of life; welcome to the supernatural!

Chapter One

The Sons Of God Are Here!

For the earnest expectation of the creature waiteth for the manifestation of the sons of God.

For we know that the whole creation groaneth and travaileth in pain together until now.

Romans 8:19,22

The whole earth has been held down, tormented, afflicted and buffeted by the devil. There are cries of oppression as humanity groans in pain, looking here and there in search of emancipation and a way out.

What the world is actually waiting for is the manifestation of the sons of God, men and women who will, by the power of God, bring deliverance and liberty to mankind. The world is waiting for sons of God who will disarm the forces of wickedness and bring the creature out of the bondage of corruption into the glorious liberty of the sons of God.

The whole creation is groaning and travailing in pain together until now, waiting for the sons of God to rescue them out of shame and reproach. Everyone that is born-again is a child of God, an heir of God, and a joint heir with Jesus.

But the whole creation is not waiting for children because children cannot exercise the dominion and authority that will result in their liberty; the world is waiting for the sons of God.

A Son Is Given

Everyone is born as a child. This is true in the natural as well as in the spiritual. However, every child has the potential of becoming a son. There is a seed of sonship implanted in everyone at birth, which will have to undergo the usual growth processes for it to mature into sonship. A child is born, but sons are given:

> ***For unto us a child is born, unto us a son is given...***
> *Isaiah 9:6*

Although everyone has the potential of becoming a son, not everyone does in reality, biological age ties notwithstanding. Many adults live as children all their lives. Such people are quite incapable of taking vital decisions or handling responsibilities. Some are married but are still ruled by their parents. Their parents tell them when to love their wives and when not to. In our culture, where there is a close link between parents and their children, this is often a source of conflict between wives and their parents-in-law.

Until a child matures into a son, he is excluded from handling certain responsibilities. Can you imagine an eight-year-old child crowned as king? No! No matter his right to the throne, he has to undergo the usual growth processes until he matures to adulthood.

> ***Now I say, That the heir, as long as he is a child, differeth nothing from a servant, though he be lord of all.***
>
> *Galatians 4:1*

God does not entrust authority to children but to sons. However, in the Church today, too many are still children, suffering the same afflictions, oppressions, failures, family crises and stagnation as the world because: *...the heir, as long as he is a child, differeth nothing from a servant, though he be Lord of all.*

An heir, who is not yet mature for his throne, will be kept under a regency, which will decide and execute decisions for him. He has no freedom or ability to exercise authority. Whatever the regency decides is good enough for him. Until he becomes mature, his authority is under "bondage." Just like in the natural, many in the Kingdom are born-again but are being robbed and cheated by the devil and his agents. This is not because they have the right to do so but because their victims refused to grow. So, Grow Up!

> ***As newborn babes, desire the sincere milk of the word, that ye may grow thereby.***
>
> *1 Peter 2:2*

Only babies feed on milk for growth. For an adult, milk is no longer essential for growth. It could be quite irritating to see a grown adult still carrying about a feeding bottle. What he needs is solid food that will give strength to his muscles.

The fact that you are born again does not give you automatic access to your Kingdom inheritance. In fact, no matter the prophecies that have gone before you, you will have to grow into them through knowledge and spiritual exercises if you must see their manifestations in your life. As long as you refuse to grow, you will live as a servant without tasting a vast portion of your inheritance in Christ. Therefore, it is not just enough to discover our heritage, those discoveries must be developed, or they might as well not exist.

Manifesting Your Sonship

Our sonship is the backbone of life in the supernatural. That is what gives us access to walk in the realm of the supernatural.

> ***But as many as received him, to them gave he power to become the sons of God, even to them that***

believe on his name.

John 1:12

The cardinal mark of sonship is power; the power to reign and exercise authority. Anyone who is born-again has this power potentially. But he can only grow into actual manifestation. Today, there are many in the church who, though born-again, hardly have anything tangible to show for their Christianity. But the truth is that they are victims of ignorance more than anything else.

Understanding your sonship power, rights and privileges is the master key to freedom and a life of fulfillment. That is what puts you over and puts the enemy on the run.

As long as Jesus emphasised His sonship, the enemy was kept restless on his toes. Just like anyone else, Jesus was not born as a son; He was born as a child but grew into His sonship.

And Jesus increased in wisdom and stature, and in favour with God and man.

Luke 2:52

Yes, Jesus was born a child like every other child, and He underwent the various growth stages. However, as soon as the voice from the clouds declared His sonship at the mount of transfiguration (Matthew 17:5), His status changed. He ascended His throne, vested with all the authority and power of heaven. Whatever He commanded came to be.

He had been enthroned, and wherever the word of a king is, there is power. Negative and positive forces were compelled to obey Him. He cast out devils with His words. A time came when He didn't even have to speak; His presence compelled evil spirits to come out of their victims. Now remember that Jesus is the pattern son; He is our perfect example, and as the Father has sent Him, so He sent you. Everything Jesus manifested as a son ought to come cheaply to you when you attain the status of sonship. That is the time you will take charge and be in control of all affairs of life.

Sometime in 1984, a lady came to me with a pathetic story of harassment by a swarm of insects. They hovered around her head and followed her everywhere she went. She was in utter embarrassment and grief. However, as she approached the entrance of the church, the insects stayed behind. After she narrated her story, I asked about the insects, and she told me they stayed back as she stepped into the gate. So I told her we should go over to see them. I took my staff to go and kill the insects, but as we headed towards the gate, they began to move backwards–it was a swarm of praying mantis. We did not need to use slings or any instruments to chase them away. They disappeared at our presence, and that was the end of that experience. Evil spirits know their bounds.

After your sonship is declared, every force in heaven and hell obeys your voice. Your status as His son commands respect in human, animal and insect kingdoms. This is what makes Christianity different. Christianity is neither a religion nor a philosophy, it does not belong to an organisation, but it is the release of the life of God into human vessels. It is becoming a member of a mysterious body from where you draw mysterious virtue to live a mysterious life.

God is committed to bringing you out of childhood into sonship so that all the forces of life will obey you. The devil will become a toy in your hand, and you will enter the fullness of your inheritance in Christ. The whole world is waiting for your manifestation.

That is precisely why I have written this book because many Christians who should be solution providers are still crying babies. Believers who should provide the answers are still locked up in sickness, poverty and all manner of satanic bondage. But that is not God's will.

God's desire for this end-time is to storm the world with the manifestation of His sons, where every man and woman in the Church is a worker of signs and wonders, where everyone will be operating on the frequency of the first-century apostles, emitting the same quality of fire, producing undeniable results.

Friend, the time has come when signs should follow your steps, causing you to leave a blazing trail of signs and wonders everywhere you go. In the days in which we live, God expects you to be an able representative of Jesus, such that anyone with a desire to see God is satisfied as he comes in contact with you because you have answers to the questions of his/her life.

That is why you must rise up vehemently against that stagnation, sickness or any other anti-covenant thing hanging around you because the husbandman must be the first partaker of the fruits. It will in fact amount to a thing of ridicule for a believer who is to lay hands on the sick to be sick himself, for one who should cast out devils to be oppressed by demons. Every unction passing through you to benefit mankind should benefit you first and foremost.

Jesus, the pattern Son, experienced all that He taught. He healed the sick and was never sick Himself. He cast out demons and was never oppressed by any. He carried virtue for prosperity and was not a pauper. Friend, if the virtues in you do not benefit you, you may well be called an ass. Remember Balaam's ass, which prophesied in Numbers 22:28-30? That will not be you, in Jesus' name!

Understand God's Miracle Plan

The world we live in is in dire need of miracles. But miracles are not accidental occurrences: they are the deliberate acts of God, motivated by the desperate faith of men. In essence, there is what to do to command a flow of miracles. There are certain things you must know to operate the miraculous.

God has a miracle plan for the Church, prepared from the foundation of the world. We see a shadow of it at creation when God made man.

Adam, before the fall, was a miracle; everything about him was extraordinary. His body was superb; hence, there was no provision for drugs; all the herbs in the garden were for food. His mind was miraculous. This was proven when he single-handedly named all the animals intelligibly, without repeating any name. His spirit was in union with God. Without a doubt, Adam enjoyed life in the miraculous.

The fall of man signalled his exit from God's miracle plan. By his act of disobedience, Adam had swapped his dominion over everything the Lord had made (his life in the miraculous inclusive) for a life of oppression. Although he was king of the earth, he sold off to Satan and legally transferred his right to live in the miraculous to Satan. Whereas previously, whatever Adam said was law, after the fall, he lost control and was no longer in charge.

For a time, it looked as if God's plan for man to walk in the miraculous had been thwarted. But the Word of the Lord came unto Isaiah saying:

> ***Therefore the Lord himself shall give you a sign; Behold, a virgin shall conceive, and bear a son, and***

shall call his name Immanuel.

Isaiah 7:14

According to the above scripture, God was talking about someone to come, whose appearing would not be hid — a sign. Later, we understood that the prophecy was about Jesus. Thus, when Jesus came to the earth, He came as a sign. By His death, Jesus stripped Satan of all His powers. He came out of the grave King of kings and Lord of lords and declared: *All power is given unto me in heaven and in earth...* He then went ahead to reinstate man in God's miracle plan.

> ***And he said unto them, Go ye into all the world, and preach the gospel to every creature.***
>
> ***He that believeth and is baptized shall be saved; but he that believeth not shall be damned.***
>
> ***And these signs shall follow them that believe; In my name shall they cast out devils; they shall speak with new tongues;***
>
> ***They shall take up serpents; and if they drink any deadly thing, it shall not hurt them; they shall lay hands on the sick, and they shall recover.***
>
> *Mark 16:15-18*

Therefore, as Jesus came to the earth as a sign, so are you a sign to the world (John 20:21). You are for signs and wonders, not sighs and sorrows. You are a sign of distinction, affluence, divine health, progress, etc. Wherever you go, according to God's miracle plan, you should be recognised as a sign carrier and wonder worker.

Friend, you are not here on earth to look for miracles because God already recognises you as a miracle! You should not be the one looking for signs; you are ordained to be a living witness of Jesus, a proof-producing Christian. The world is waiting for answers from us, but when we do not know how to obtain answers ourselves, how shall we provide answers for them?

That is why I think a Christian should be ashamed of sickness the way he is of sin. He should be embarrassed at defeat or failure in his life the way he would be at being caught in adultery. This is because by virtue of his new status in Christ, he should not be under anything anymore. So, God is upset when you are cheated, defeated and manhandled because on His part, He has done all He needs to do to ensure you live a victorious life.

Signs Are Your Heritage

Signs are the heritage of all believers; two scriptures validate this:

> ***Behold, I and the children whom the Lord hath given me are for signs and for wonders in Israel from the Lord of hosts, which dwelleth in mount Zion.***
>
> *Isaiah 8:18*

And these signs shall follow them that believe; In my name shall they cast out devils; they shall speak with new tongues;

They shall take up serpents; and if they drink any deadly thing, it shall not hurt them; they shall lay hands on the sick, and they shall recover.

Mark 16:17-18

A sign is something beyond the ordinary; it authenticates the involvement of God in an issue. It comes by the finger of God, something beyond human ability; a proof of God's omnipotence! God says signs shall follow you! That is simply amazing! It means God wants to make you a monument, a beacon of hope in a dark world and clear evidence to the entire world around you that you are a believer. Remember, *And these signs shall follow them that believe...*

Therefore, by virtue of your status, you are to be followed by signs, not sorrows. The devil himself is under your feet, so wherever you appear, he must disappear! However, until you can grasp the reality of your heritage in God, you can never walk in the miraculous.

Some time ago, a woman told me that, for some inexplicable reasons, the clothing materials she was selling were not being bought. I went to her shop, laid my hands on the merchandise and said, "Clothes, be gone, now!" The following day, some people came from outside the town, and they bought up everything!

On another occasion, a brother came to tell me that the items in his shop were also not being bought. I laid my hands on his hands and declared, "Go back to your store and lay these hands on those materials." He went down to his shop and did the same. To his amazement, the following day, at about twelve noon, a man reversed his trailer into his drive way and purchased every item in the shop! Thereafter, I said to myself, "Imagine if that brother were the owner of my hands? It would simply be a matter of touching his goods every morning and going to sleep."

But in actual fact, he has access to the same miracle hands I have, and so does everyone that believes. Unfortunately, not all believers know there is a miracle in their hands. They think it is only in the hands of the pastors, evangelists or bishops, but it is the heritage of every child of God!

Friend, there is something in your hands that can produce answers for mankind and should be able to produce answers for you too. So much has been invested into you, but your discovery of those treasures will lead to your recovery in life and determine how much results you produce.

Chapter Two

Reality Of The Supernatural

Two main forces dominate the supernatural world. They are God and the devil, the forces of good and evil. These two forces cannot be compared in any way. One is greater and mightier than the other. God is the Almighty, the source of all powers. He is life; He is existence itself. He created the devil, and it is impossible for the creature to be as or more powerful than the creator. However, God did not create the devil as the evil one he now is. He was created as the angel of light, a perfect being.

> ***Son of man, take up a lamentation upon the king of Tyrus, and say unto him, Thus saith the Lord GOD; Thou sealest up the sum, full of wisdom, and perfect in beauty.***
>
> ***Thou hast been in Eden the garden of God; every***

precious stone was thy covering, the sardius, topaz, and the diamond, the beryl, the onyx, and the jasper, the sapphire, the emerald, and the carbuncle, and gold: the workmanship of thy tabrets and of thy pipes was prepared in thee in the day that thou wast created.

Thou art the anointed cherub that covereth; and I have set thee so: thou wast upon the holy mountain of God; thou hast walked up and down in the midst of the stones of fire.

Thou wast perfect in thy ways from the day that thou wast created, till iniquity was found in thee.

Ezekiel 28:12-15

Lucifer was excellent in all his ways until sin was found in him. What sin did he commit? He wanted to rise up to the skies. He wanted to take the position of the most High, his creator.

How art thou fallen from heaven, O Lucifer, son of the morning! how art thou cut down to the ground, which didst weaken the nations!

For thou hast said in thine heart, I will ascend into heaven, I will exalt my throne above the stars of God: I will sit also upon the mount of the congregation, in the sides of the north:

I will ascend above the heights of the clouds; I will be like the most High.

Isaiah 14:12-14

He was created and called Lucifer, the son of the morning. The name Lucifer means "the shining one." He was one of the three mighty princes that exercised authority over the other angels. They were all a spirit race of beings created by God. When Lucifer sinned, he was dethroned. He was cast down from heaven, and from that moment, the devil emerged. He started his mission of countering everything God created.

God did not create evil; everything He created was declared good and very good. The devil himself did not create anything. All he did was embark on his mission of reversing God's creation. Good was reversed, and evil emerged. Truth was turned around, and lies appeared on the scene. Love was reverted, and hatred emerged. Sweet was turned to sweat, and abundance to poverty, etc. This was entirely the devil's doing. Before the fall of Lucifer, there was only one governing force in the universe, but after his revolt, two forces came to be.

Man's Dethronement To The Natural Realm

Man was created by God in His own image and likeness and put in a perfect setting – the garden of Eden. Satan, in his characteristic way, sought to dethrone him. As long as man was in the garden, Satan had no control over him. He was frustrated by this setup and wanted to surround God's man with every evil he could think of, but he could not because man was out of his reach in the garden.

Satan knew that the only way man could be driven out of the garden into his hands was through disobedience and sin. He knew that God could not stand sin, and God's relationship with man could be severed if man sinned. So he sought to make man disobey God.

He succeeded through his subtlety. He went through the woman and deceived her, and she involved her husband. They ate the forbidden fruit, and their eyes were opened. They were not physically blind, but they entered into a negative phase of existence. God's judgement for disobedience is death, and Man died. It was not physical annihilation; he still retained his consciousness and moved about the garden, but the vital force that sustained him was gone.

With his death, he lost his throne and placement. He became subject to the things that were once subject to him. Man became miserable. Man disobeyed God through Satan's trickery, and like Satan, he was chased out of the Garden of Eden. Then the reign of terror began. Man was afflicted with all manner of evil by the evil one.

God's perfect man became the devil's meat. However, this was not the end of man. God is still the overall ruling power. Satan is only engaged in a battle, which he has been divinely ordained to lose. He knows this, for his time is short – ... *art thou come hither to torment us before the time?* (Matthew 8: 29). He knows his end. He is only trying to cause as much havoc as he can before the time comes for his final demise.

These two forces dominate the supernatural. You are either in one camp or the other. There is no middle way between the two. You are either connected to the good source – God or you are connected to the evil source – the devil. Where you are connected to determines the realm in which you operate.

If you are tuned in to God, you operate in the power of the Holy Spirit through Christ Jesus. You will be operating in the good realm, releasing blessings upon yourself and others. On the other hand, if you are tuned in to the devil, you will be operating through demons in the evil realm. You will be releasing magic, curses and destruction upon yourself and others.

Satan's Magnetic Field

The Bible is full of evidence of the reality of an evil world under the control of Satan. It is a dark world in which Satan freely inflicts evil on those under his control. Apostle John brings us to an awareness of this fact in 1 John 5:19:

> ***And we know that we are of God, and the whole world lieth in wickedness.***

The entire world lies in a magnetic field of wickedness,

where Satan, his demons and sometimes human extensions carry out their wicked acts by remote control. Diseases, frustrations and all kinds of human afflictions originate here. Spells and curses that upturn people's destinies come from this negative pole of evil. A satanic influence is almost always behind the stagnation, failures and losses people experience in life.

The sad thing is that because of ignorance and sometimes insensitivity, many Christians become vulnerable to the wickedness of the devil. Many are diligent, but only a few are vigilant. Many are sincere, but only a few are sensitive. So don't be deceived. If Satan attempted Christ, the Son of God, he would attempt to control anyone else. The truth is that every accomplishment of destiny attracts the devil's attention. He will do everything to frustrate it. He chased Moses out into the wilderness for 40 years.

The drama at the court of Pharaoh between Moses and the magicians of Pharaoh is typical of the contest between good and evil. Just like the rod of Moses swallowed up the magicians' rods, so do the forces of good always overcome the forces of evil. The satanic world is always counterfeiting the real thing. Such counterfeits are designed to intimidate, deceive and distract from the truth. No Christian must be so foolish to be deceived by them.

Elijah's encounter with the prophets of Baal was another contest between the forces of good and evil.

Elijah had challenged them:

> ***...Call ye on the name of your gods, and I will call on the name of the LORD: and the God that answereth by fire, let him be God.***
>
> *1 Kings 18:24*

When the chips were down, the God of Elijah won. God proved His sovereignty by sending down fire at Elijah's instance. God will always have the last action, no matter the roar and threat of the devil.

The mysterious escape of the three Hebrew children from Nebuchadnezzar's fiery furnace is typical of God's deliverance for every believer, who will not compromise his faith in the face of severe opposition and attack of the enemy. The climax of the contest was that between Christ and Satan. From infancy, he sought to eliminate Him. He entered into king Herod, and countless number of innocent children were killed. However, at the cross, Christ humiliated him. His death and resurrection brought an eternal defeat to Satan.

With that, Satan was stripped of all powers. Understand this: Satan does not have all the powers attributed to him. No! All powers belong to God, whose you are. What he has left is deception. So get this into your consciousness, and you will be set free from all anxiety and fears. Don't be scared of Satan's roarings and threats. You live in a superior positive realm in which Christ and the angels of God reign and are on standby to establish your victory.

> ***For whatsoever is born of God overcometh the world: and this is the victory that overcometh the world, even our faith.***
>
> *1 John 5:4*

By covenant, you are an overcomer. The whole world may lie in wickedness, but you will be exempted from it if you remain in God. If you are conscious of your redemptive placement in Christ, you are automatically outside the satanic magnetic field. You have been translated from the kingdom of darkness to the Kingdom of light, where the devil and his spiritual and human hosts of wickedness cannot reach you.

Man Is Re-Enthroned!

Jesus came on an everlasting mission to restore man to the life of God, which Adam lost to Satan. The Bible announced the mission of Jesus in John 3:16:

> ***For God so loved the world, that he gave his only begotten Son, that whosoever believeth in him should not perish, but have everlasting life.***

Before Jesus came, man was in a perishing state; stripped of all honour, dignity and power. He lost control of every aspect of life. The natural man, the man without Jesus in his life, is under the control of the evil one.

Without Christ, you are in a state of perishing under Satan's reign of terror; he does what he likes with you and can link you up with any demon of his choice. That is why you find men addicted to cigarette smoking that even when the doctor warns them about its risks to their health, they can't stop. They try to, but a stronger force than them prevents them from victory. Isn't it obvious that such persons are perishing?

> ***Jesus told the Syrophenician woman, It is not meet to take the children's bread and cast it unto the dogs.***
>
> *Mark 7:27*

The children of God are only those who have received divine nature through Christ. Those who reject Christ are no better than dogs. That is how God regards them. It sounds unfair, but that is what the Word of God says.

Only through Christ can anyone enter the covenant and be rescued from perishing. Through Christ, God once again re-establishes man in his position of dominion, where he has control over all things. Man can once again live supernaturally on the earth. This means living out of the ordinary through divine motivation. But how does this operate? How does one step from the natural into the supernatural?

Chapter Three

The New Birth Command

That which is born of the flesh is flesh; and that which is born of the Spirit is spirit.

Marvel not that I said unto thee, Ye must be born again.

John 3:6-7

Everyone who is born-again is born a sign. Nobody can tell where he is going or coming from. His ways become past finding out, just as it is with God. He becomes a walking miracle, operating signs naturally and at will.

The new birth brings you into a new sphere of existence where you cease from being a struggling human being to a commander of signs and wonders. That is why that scripture says:

The wind bloweth where it listeth...

You flow in realms where you have things the way you want them.

The Mystery of Regeneration

When you accept Jesus as your Lord and Saviour, something significant happens to you. The Bible explains it thus:

> ***Therefore if any man be in Christ, he is a new creature: old things are passed away; behold, all things are become new.***
>
> *2 Corinthians 5:17*

The new birth is described as being in Christ Jesus. When you consciously step out of Satan's fold and accept Jesus as your Lord and Saviour, He comes into your heart and gives you a new life. Your old nature passes away, and the new nature of Christ Jesus is born in you.

You are then referred to as being born-again by the Spirit of God. You become a new creature with God's supernatural nature inside of you. You can now live supernaturally. With the power of God at work in you, you can now live out of the ordinary. How do you show forth the supernatural nature of God in you?

Some years ago, I had a rare opportunity to manifest the supernatural nature of God in me, and it was exciting. There was this young lady who was possessed of the devil and was upsetting her entire family. She enthroned herself as a little tin god, driving her parents to a state of despair by her constant evil manifestations, and they could do nothing about it.

One day, the Spirit of God came very heavily upon me, and I (in the company of another brother) put her in a van and drove to an unknown road in the valley. This was very late at night, so when we got out of the car, I said to her, "Whatever I tell you to do, do it. Now lie flat..." She obeyed, shivering like a leaf. I was issuing commands to her, and she was obeying without question.

I was full of power from the knowledge that I am above the devil, and when I am talking, he must keep quiet. I further asked, "Why has your master not come to rescue you from my hands? Do they not call him the prince of the power of darkness? Where is he now?" Her answer was most revealing. She said, "As long as you are here, he cannot come." I had the power to destroy her with no devil coming to her rescue because my God is the God of the day and the night.

Also, some years back, I needed to go out early in the morning, so I went to start my car. The only response I got was a horrible noise from the engine. My well-meaning neighbour heard it too and came over to us (I had a visiting co-minister and personal friend with me then) and said, "Sir, it appears your car engine is about to knock." I came out of the car, opened the bonnet and in the name of Jesus, I commanded the engine-knocking demon to get off my car. This was promptly obeyed and supposedly landed on my well-meaning neighbour's car, which packed up within a week! He had to do without his car for six months!

This is out of the ordinary. This is living by engaging divine forces. This is extraordinary. At new birth, the believer steps out of the ordinary into the extraordinary. The first time Jesus mentioned being born-again was related to supernatural living, as revealed in His encounter with Nicodemus. As a matter of fact, that is the major identification mark of the new birth.

To Nicodemus' question, Jesus answered:

> ***...Except a man be born again, he cannot see the kingdom of God.***
>
> ***...Except a man be born of water and of the Spirit, he cannot enter into the kingdom of God.***
>
> ***That which is born of the flesh is flesh; and that which is born of the Spirit is spirit.***
>
> ***Marvel not that I said unto thee, Ye must be born again.***
>
> ***The wind bloweth where it listeth, and thou hearest the sound thereof, but canst not tell whence it cometh, and whither it goeth: so is every one that is born of the Spirit.***
>
> *John 3:3, 6-8*

Those born of the Spirit of God belong to the extraordinary class of people. They call divine forces into operation like the wind. They blow like the wind and operate outside of the ordinary. They call divine forces into operation, and you only see the resultant effects, but you don't see and cannot tell how the operation was carried out. Jesus said that the man born of the Spirit operates like the wind. You cannot tell from where the wind comes and where it is going. You only hear the sound. The "sound" of the children of God is not an ordinary sound; it is a sound from the spirit that is backed with heavenly energy, carrying effectively whatever orders the saint gives.

If you are born of the Spirit, you are designed to live this order of life. It is not meant for a privileged few; this supernatural life is for everyone born of the Spirit of God. There is nothing like the gift of heaven; heaven is for everyone who has received Jesus as Lord and Saviour.

Get this clear: if you are born of the Spirit, the supernatural life is for you. You are to exhibit that supernatural nature of God in you in your daily life. The entire world believes there is no mountain a miracle cannot make plain. It accepts the ability of a miracle to deal with any situation. It takes a miracle to come out of critical situations. What is a miracle? It is the supernatural intervention of God. This is what you are – a miracle. You are the supernatural intervention the world needs to get out of difficult situations. This is the manifestation of the supernatural life in you.

Ye Are Gods

In God's order of creation, every living thing produces after its kind. The original creature simply duplicates itself in its offspring. Thus, a dog can only give birth to a dog; it cannot give birth to a goat. The same applies to plant life. A mango tree can only produce mangoes, not oranges. That is the principle.

Now at the creation of man, God subjected himself to the same principle of life. He used Himself as the original and spoke man into existence from His very self.

> ***And God said, Let us make man in our image, after our likeness...***
>
> *Genesis 1:26*

Since the scripture cannot be broken, not even by God, the same principle of life obtained at the creation of other things came into force. God was duplicated in man, leaving man with all divine attributes that would make him operate like the true son of his Father. Adam operated fully in the class of God. He had fellowship with him. God visited him from time to time to find out how he was administering the Garden of Eden.

He was endowed with the wisdom of God, and that enabled him to stand in his position as the caretaker of God's other creation. Consider how he called the other animals to himself and gave them names. That takes wisdom and authority. Like God, Adam was also endowed with creative potentials. He was created to be fruitful and to reproduce himself. However, as established, when man fell, he lost his divine attributes. The essence of the divine was lost, and man became mere flesh. Thenceforward, human beings gave birth to human beings. Like will always beget like.

Your New Status

Let me quickly state that spiritual laws or principles will always work whether you know them or not, whether you agree with them or not. Not everyone born of man is a child of God. When Jesus was here; occasion, he had to tell the Jews, who by ancestry were children of Abraham.

> ***Ye are of your father the devil, and the lusts of your father ye will do…***
>
> *John 8:44*

Since the fall, what makes anyone a child of God is the new birth. That is the spiritual initiation that reestablishes the divine nature in any man. When you come to Jesus, a spiritual rebirth which necessitates a spiritual transfer takes place. The Spirit of God through Jesus is born in you. Then you are said to be born again. You become a new creature, and new growth (in the spiritual realm) starts in you.

> ***Jesus answered, Verily, verily, I say unto thee, Except a man be born of water and of the Spirit, he***

> ***cannot enter into the kingdom of God.***
>
> ***That which is born of the flesh is flesh; and that which is born of the Spirit is spirit.***
>
> *John 3:5-6*

Being born of the Spirit makes you a spirit. Jesus said *That which is born of the Spirit is spirit.* Note that He did not say, "That which is born of the spirit is spiritual." No! You are not spiritual, you are only called to be spiritually minded, and your mind is part of your flesh. That is why you are asked to give it a new orientation now that the real you has come alive.

By virtue of new birth, you belong to a higher order of the spirit realm. For instance, it won't take me too much effort to destroy a witch because I am higher and stronger. Thus, I have the power to destroy the weaker being. The supernatural world is the spirit world. God expects you to be alive and alert in the spirit all the time.

> ***God is a Spirit: and they that worship him must worship him in spirit and in truth.***
>
> *John 4:24*

If you must worship Him profitably, you must do so in spirit and in truth. Your worship of Him must be in the spirit and not the flesh because He cannot be stirred up into action by your flesh except by your spirit. It is your spirit-man that relates with Him. Thus, how alive your spirit is what determines how much you count before

Him and how much of a meaningful relationship you can enjoy with Him. Then, if God be spirit, those born of Him cannot be flesh because the law of reproduction demands that like beget like.

Your Divine Nature

The strongest opposition the Jews had against the Ministry of Jesus was His proclamation of His father-son relationship with God. They could not stand it because it provoked them to the extent that they sought to kill Him many times.

> ***Then the Jews took up stones again to stone him.***
>
> ***Jesus answered them, Many good works have I shewed you from my Father; for which of those works do ye stone me?***
>
> ***The Jews answered him, saying, For a good work we stone thee not; but for blasphemy; and because that thou, being a man, makest thyself God.***
>
> *John 10:31-33*

Jesus could not be daunted by their threats; He knew who He was and where He came from. Besides, He knew the scriptures and what they said about the God-man relationship. He knew that children of God are gods.

> ***I have said, Ye are gods; and all of you are children of the most High.***
>
> *Psalm 82:6*

The believers are the ones to whom, when the word of God came, believed, and by believing, they became children of God. The Father called them gods.

> ***If he called them gods, unto whom the word of God came, and the scripture cannot be broken.***
>
> *John 10:35*

If sons of men are men, then sons of God are gods. Just like children have the attributes of their natural parents, so do the children of God have the attributes of God. No matter how fond you are of your pet, it can never be called your child. You are not in the same class of being; it can never manifest your attributes in spite of your fondness.

If you are born-again, you must accept your divine nature. The human nature is associated with humanity, while the divine nature is associated with God. Just like human nature makes man, human, divine nature makes God, God. A genuinely born-again person has the divine nature inside him.

The reason many believers have not come to terms fully with this truth is that we have stayed so long among humans. We are so body-oriented, conscious largely of operations within our five senses. We have come to believe there is no difference between the rest of humanity and us. We live in the same communities, we shop together, work together etc.

During one of my meetings in one of the northern

cities of Nigeria, I visited one of the elders of our church whose goat demonstrates the powerful effect of association on behaviour. The goat had been reared with his dog. Over time, the goat began to behave exactly like a dog.

When its master returned home from work, like the dog, it wagged its tail as a sign of welcome. But much more disturbing, the goat no longer feeds on leaves or vegetables; it feeds on whatever the dog feeds on, including excreta! I never read this from any book or heard it from anybody; I witnessed it.

Association has robbed believers of the consciousness of their divine nature; you will never be in control of the affairs of life if you keep the wrong company. God did not programme you to live and die like men (that is, live unfulfilled and unaccomplished lives), but He programmed you for distinction. He loaded you with divine abilities and potentials that would make you operate in His class and exercise dominion over the affairs of life. That may be regarded as blasphemous, but that explains the human predicament.

Until you embrace the truth of your divine nature, don't expect to be in control. You will be buffeted and suffer like ordinary men. A revelation of your divine nature will open you up to the realm of the supernatural. When you become consciously aware of this truth, even when you are asleep, the wicked forces on earth would cheaply surrender to you.

There was a time my wife was admitted to the hospital and was on drips for a supposedly serious attack. When I got to the hospital, I told the doctor to remove the drips and discharge her. He looked at me in amazement, but I had my way. Later that day, she still attended the end-of-year pastors' banquet. That ended the affliction.

Sometime ago, my youngest daughter was said to have tuberculosis. When the news got to me, I simply said, "No, it can't happen!" and forgot about it. I dismissed it as guesswork. Praise God, the same doctor who had earlier diagnosed tuberculosis came back with the report that it had left.

The consciousness of your divine nature will change your attitude towards life and things. You will be so settled about issues of life that when men run helter-skelter, you will be at peace. Jesus knew who He was, so even in the midst of a storm, while His disciples were frantically wearing themselves out in their bid to save their lives, He could afford to sleep. When He finally woke up, He calmed the storms with His words. Jesus could afford to sleep because He was conscious of His position in God. Throughout the New Testament, Jesus kept saying, "I and my Father are one; if you see me, you have seen my Father," etc.

Believers need to be conscious of this fact too. God did not call you a man; He called you a god. So get your thinking tuned into this.

The First Adam

Before the fall, Adam operated in the class of God; his mind functioned in the same frequency as God's. He was a man of authority, a man of dominion. However, one day, he ate the forbidden fruit, and in accordance with God's warning, he died.

Adam's death was spiritual, not physical. He was still physically alive, but his spirit was disconnected from God. At that very instance, he went from the realm of the supernatural to the natural. He descended from the spirit world to the physical world. He also became a victim of what he used to have dominion over.

But God was undaunted, and as in a relay race, He picked up the baton Adam had dropped and passed it unto Jesus, who did not fail Him.

Jesus came primarily to recreate what had died in Adam — his spirit. He came to restore to humanity what had been lost in Adam. He was called the second Adam because, like the first Adam, He was a representative of all mankind. With this restoration, as many as receive Jesus into their hearts can operate in the same class as the first Adam before the fall.

> ***And so it is written, The first man Adam was made a living soul; the last Adam was made a quickening spirit.***
>
> ***Howbeit that was not first which is spiritual, but that which is natural; and afterward that which is***

spiritual.

The first man is of the earth, earthy: the second man is the Lord from heaven.

1 Corinthians 15:45-47

The new birth is much more than merely responding to an altar call. It could start from there, but until you have an in-depth understanding of your new status, reflecting the heavenly life will be a mere dream.

I pray that your understanding is opened, and then such statements as, "Under this circumstance, what can I do as a human being?" will no longer come out of your mouth! Please be aware of your new status in Christ; it is the beginning of your journey into life in the miraculous.

But ye are a chosen generation, a royal priesthood, an holy nation, a peculiar people; that ye should show forth the praises of him who hath called you out of darkness into his marvellous light:

1 Peter 2:9

This scripture gives credence to the fact that we are new creatures, belonging to a royal priesthood and chosen to show forth His praise. We have no cause to fear what men of the world fear — for we are not of the world, our citizenship is of heaven. We belong to a superior sphere and a higher cadre of life.

Many people say, "You know in this world, you can't be sure of anything," "There are wicked men all around," etc. Because you are a peculiar person, made for signs and wonders, created not only to be different but to make a difference in this world, you can be sure of yourself. This mentality must engulf you if you are to take charge and be in full command of life's situations.

It was this consciousness that inspired Jesus to say:

> ***...My kingdom is not of this world: if my kingdom were of this world, then would my servants fight, that I should not be delivered to the Jews: but now is my kingdom not from hence.***
>
> *John 18:36*

He knew where He was coming from, so it was easy for Him to maintain His territory and retain His status. If you can key into this revelation, you will no longer be subject to the harassment of the devil.

Your Superiority Over The Devil

> ***Who hath delivered us from the power of darkness, and hath translated us into the kingdom of his dear Son:***
>
> *Colossians 1:13*

Once you are born-again, you are translated or transferred from the kingdom of darkness into the Kingdom of God's dear Son. The forces of darkness no longer have power over you; the weeping, mourning and gnashing of teeth that are characteristic of Satan's kingdom cease in your life. The moment you are born-again, you are no longer in the kingdom of tears but cheers. Your sorrow is turned into joy, your weeping to laughter!

The devil's government has a constitution. John10:10 describes it as:

The thief cometh not, but for to steal, and to kill, and to destroy...

But as soon as you give your life to Christ, you are no longer under the devil's government. So his evil desires, schemes, wiles and devices have no legal hold on you; you have been redeemed by the blood of the Lamb.

And there was war in heaven: Michael and his angels fought against the dragon; and the dragon fought and his angels,

And prevailed not; neither was their place found any more in heaven.

And the great dragon was cast out, that old serpent, called the Devil, and Satan, which deceiveth the whole world: he was cast out into the earth, and his angels were cast out with him.

And I heard a loud voice saying in heaven, Now is come salvation, and strength, and the kingdom of our God, and the power of his Christ: for the accuser of our brethren is cast down, which accused them before our God day and night.

And they overcame him by the blood of the Lamb, and by the word of their testimony; and they loved

not their lives unto the death.

Therefore rejoice, ye heavens, and ye that dwell in them. Woe to the inhabiters of the earth and of the sea! for the devil is come down unto you, having great wrath, because he knoweth that he hath but a short time.

Revelation 12:7-12

Satan could not prevail in heaven, so he was cast down to the earth. Two kingdoms are brought to light here; the earthly and heavenly. Only those who reside in the earthly kingdom are under the wrath of Satan. Those who are born-again have been translated from the earthly to the heavenly Kingdom. And there is rejoicing in the heavenly Kingdom because there is no place found for Satan there anymore.

As a new creature in Christ, we can safely conclude that Satan has no right to be anywhere around you. Therefore, in your heavenly citizen status, you should be able to display "the riches of His glory" in the face of the devil, not suffering as those in earthly places do. Just like Enoch, who was translated and did not see death, you have been translated too, so you do not experience the same buffeting as the world.

The fact that you have been redeemed guarantees you absolute liberty from all forms of oppression of the devil. You are no longer his captive, so he cannot plague your body or tamper with the works of your hand. This knowledge should spur you into reacting against the gimmicks of hell in all areas of your life.

Everybody may be complaining about the devil, but God is complaining about the ignorance of His people! Sometimes ago, by inspiration, I said there is no mountain anywhere; every man's ignorance is his mountain. Those cases that look special are really not special; many only have a case of "special" ignorance! Once you know where you belong, you should be able to confront the devil and secure your victory.

For instance, sickness is not your portion in God. So, if you sense an attack of sickness coming, react against it based on the light of God's Word you have contacted. Don't nurse or accept it; just fight it off and enjoy liberty.

I perceive very strongly in my spirit that God will bring a lot of revelations on the weakness of Satan our way this end-time. Just like ants in a man's house do not pose a problem to his existence, Satan is not your problem; you can handle him!

Many years ago, my cousin, who is a medical doctor, tested my blood pressure and said, "Oh, your blood pressure is high!" I quickly replied, "Not me." He said, "Look at it," but I did not, then I told him, "I cannot have high blood pressure." I could say that confidently because I understood we were both operating from two different realms. After then, I never prayed about it, and it was not an issue of concern. By insight about my divine status, high blood pressure was swallowed up in victory.

The advantage Satan has over believers is ignorance. He plays on the ignorance of the saints to buffet, oppress and punish them.

> ***Lest Satan should get an advantage of us: for we are not ignorant of his devices.***
>
> *2 Corinthians 2:11*

But Satan has been stripped of all his powers and is left with only wiles and devices (Ephesians 6:11).

By being conscious of your superiority over Satan, you can "take him for a ride." Instead of living at his mercy, you can turn the tables on him, compelling him to take to his heels at the mention of your name! The testimony of the demon who attacked the sons of Sceva was "Jesus I know, Paul I know." So he recognised that those were not folks to play around with. That will be Satan's testimony concerning you too!

Redemption guarantees your total liberty. With this understanding, you hold in your hands the master key to rest in all spheres of life.

The Mystery Of Identification

> ***For he hath made him to be sin for us, who knew no sin; that we might be made the righteousness of God in him.***
>
> *2 Corinthians 5:21*

Jesus took the place of man in sin, sickness, poverty, death and every evil thing in the world. He was made sin on the cross, identifying with man in the fallen state. He became sin for us.

If you are to operate in the realm of the miraculous, you must be fully aware of your identification with Christ in every stage of His redemptive work. You were in Christ in every stage of it. You were legally present there, defeating the devil when Jesus died. You took part in His suffering (His passion), His crucifixion, burial and resurrection. He became identified with you on the cross, and you with Him.

> ***Know ye not, that so many of us as were baptized into Jesus Christ were baptized into his death?***
>
> ***Therefore we are buried with him by baptism into death: that like as Christ was raised up from the dead by the glory of the Father, even so we also should walk in newness of life.***
>
> ***For if we have been planted together in the likeness of his death, we shall be also in the likeness of his resurrection:***
>
> ***Knowing this, that our old man is crucified with him, that the body of sin might be destroyed, that henceforth we should not serve sin.***
>
> *Romans 6:3-6*

When Jesus was made alive by the Spirit, you were also. You were raised up from the dead together with

Him on the basis of identification.

> ***And hath raised us up together, and made us sit together in heavenly places in Christ Jesus:***
>
> *Ephesians 2:6*

And when God raised Him up and exalted Him far above principalities and powers, you were there with Him, exalted as well. As a result of this mystery of identification, all principalities and powers are under your feet.

> ***Which he wrought in Christ, when he raised him from the dead, and set him at his own right hand in the heavenly places,***
>
> ***Far above all principality, and power, and might, and dominion, and every name that is named, not only in this world, but also in that which is to come:***
>
> ***And hath put all things under his feet, and gave him to be the head over all things to the church,***
>
> ***Which is his body, the fulness of him that filleth all in all.***
>
> *Ephesians 1:20-23*

A sound understanding of your identification with Christ will produce outstanding manifestations.

Among all the disciples of Jesus, John, the beloved, was unique. Church history tells us that when the Church was mercilessly persecuted, John was dropped into a drum of boiling oil, yet, he could not "fry" and could not be burnt. In exasperation, he was banished to the Isles of Patmos.

Behind this disciple's outstanding manifestations was the unique insight he had into the mystery of identification. In all his books, John kept referring to "The Father." He heard Jesus make those statements in reference to His identification with the Father and subsequently linked them up to the saints. Likewise, when you understand this mystery as well, you will become a sign in your community, displaying the power of God.

> ***I and my Father are one.***
>
> ***Then the Jews took up stones again to stone him.***
>
> ***Jesus answered them, Many good works have I shewed you from my Father; for which of those works do ye stone me?***
>
> ***The Jews answered him, saying, For a good work we stone thee not; but for blasphemy; and because that thou, being a man, makest thyself God.***
>
> *John 10:30-33*

No one could deny the works Jesus did, not even the skeptical Jews; He was a fountain of signs and wonders. However, behind Jesus' amazing manifestations was His keen understanding of His identification with the Father. As I often say, you cannot identify with God without proofs. Thus, Jesus produced undeniable evidence as a result of His union with God.

Here is how you come in: salvation brings you into union with God. You were previously separated from Him by sin, but now through the atoning Blood of Jesus, you have been brought back into fellowship with God. He is now your Father (John 20:17).

You are now one with the Father as Jesus was one with Him. As a result, you have the same nature as God the Father. Therefore, whatever God can handle, by virtue of identification with Christ, you can too! A good understanding of this mystery enables you to exercise your authority without fear or compromise.

> ***For as the Father hath life in himself; so hath he given to the Son to have life in himself;***
>
> ***And hath given him authority to execute judgment also, because he is the Son of man.***
>
> *John 5:26-27*

Authority answers to identification. You can execute judgement even against death. You say to it, "Shut up there!" and it respects your voice. That is how Paul cheaply dealt with death. He often mused whether to go to be with the Lord or to stay, but then he chose to stay. Jesus also could not be threatened by death. Until His hour came, no man could touch Him. He said He had the power to lay down His life and to take it up. That is authority!

A brother mistakenly drank acid, but was delivered. Here is his testimony:

About a week to my wedding, I got late to the office at about 11 a.m., and I came in very thirsty, so headed straight for the laboratory to drink from the de-ionised water (a chemically treated water), not knowing the water had been tested acidic.

I took a cup and was already drinking it when the chemist in charge of the laboratory screamed at the top of his voice, "Acid! Acid! You are drinking acid." It immediately occurred to me that I was face-to-face with death, and I remembered the scripture that says, "...declare thou, that thou mayest be justified" (Isaiah 43:26). I knew right away that my declaration at that time was the only thing that would save me.

I immediately shouted, "No! It cannot be acid. It is water." To convince me of what he was saying, the chemist tested the content of my cup, and it was negative. But when he tested the content in the container I took from, it was positive, confirming that it was acidic. Everybody was surprised, and they said, "This is not an ordinary man!" I return all the glory to God! **—Adeyeye S.**

That is eternal life on display! It conferred on him the authority to execute judgement against death.

Therefore, *...As the Father hath life in himself; so hath he given to the Son to have life in himself;* and *whosoever believeth in him should not perish, but have eternal life* (John 5:26; 3:16). By the mystery of identification, what you carry now is eternal life. You have the life of God inside you as a gift from heaven. That life cannot be terminated by any ploy of hell; it can swallow up disease, failure, stagnation, frustration and even death.

This kind of life is also known as everlasting life; that is, the life that lasts forever. The life that can't be stopped, an unending life. That life is superior to human, animal, plant or satanic life.

Some time ago, we camped in a secondary school surrounded by a thick bush, and there was this huge young man who had just been delivered from insanity. Somehow, the demons found their way back into him, and he became very violent. The heftiest brothers in the camp were the only ones who could pin him down. I was asleep in one of the rooms, but someone came to wake me up and told me what was happening.

When I got there, I was furious and instructed the brothers to leave the demoniac alone. Pointing my finger at him, I quoted from the book of Jude: *And the angels which kept not their first estate, but left their own habitation, he hath reserved in everlasting chains under darkness unto the judgment of the great day.* I then asked the devil in him, "What are you doing here?"

Immediately those words went out of my lips, he heaved a deep sigh of relief, and all the devils fled, never to return again. The man had very little education and could not have understood the words I spoke, and those words were not "grammar" but life (John 6:63)

The eternal life you carry on your inside is real; it is not theoretical. It is the exact type in Jesus that made Him immune to sickness and disease. That same life guaranteed His rest even in adverse situations. In it lay all He would ever require to live an abundant life. This same life is what you carry inside you! Once you become conscious of it, sickness cannot survive in your body. Failure itself cannot come near you.

"Drunk" with this insight, John G. Lake performed some amazing feats. He was in South Africa when a plague broke out, and thousands of people died. Lake challenged the doctors to take some of the foam from the mouths of the victims and examine it to be sure the germs were still alive. He then told them to put the foam on his hand, after which it was re-examined under a microscope. Behold, all the germs were discovered dead!

Truly, the Bible says whatsoever is born of God (a carrier of eternal life) overcomes all the hurdles of life (1 John 5:4). This truth will establish you as a celebrated miracle worker — a man licensed of God to displace the devil in any environment you step into. Not guessing, but too sure of whom you are in Christ and what God has done in you.

Ask yourself these questions: "Could Jesus be on earth now and be stranded? If He were married to your wife or husband, would He be quarrelling and fighting with His spouse? If He were riding in a car, would He be involved in an accident and be trapped under the vehicle with some villagers helping to pull His legs out of the wreck? Would He be sick and be on admission in a hospital somewhere with a nurse punching His body with a needle?"

If your answer to all these questions is no, then know it is not God's plan for you either. Jesus was an epitome of eternal life; He was eternal life in person. So, look at Jesus, compare yourself with Him and see whether you measure up to God's expectations or not. If we have the life He has, we should have the proofs He had!

Remember that at the age of twelve, with eternal life at work in Him, the doctors of law were amazed at the wisdom Jesus spoke with. He had not even been baptised in the Holy Ghost then, yet, His mind was sharp! He displayed mental soundness, such as was in Adam before the fall; this was because He was connected to the same source of life Adam was connected to.

That is why it is an insult for a man with ordinary human life to beat a man with eternal life in any examination or interview! Being born-again is a spiritual reality with earthly evidence!

Friend, you must appreciate your privileged position in God's end-time miracle plan. You are an arrow in the hands of God, which He will release this end-time to torment all the forces of darkness.

In summary, let me reiterate that the way God made Moses a god to Pharaoh is the same way He made Jesus and has, in like manner, made us gods to our generation. This understanding helped me appreciate what God said to me sometime in 1981.

One day, I was in God's presence, receiving instructions on how to run the commission, when I took up my pen and wrote my wife. In that letter, I said, "Jerusalem is in pain, our mother is in travail, the whole creation is groaning, awaiting Zion to manifest her sons. Prisoners are awaiting their emancipation. Zion shall not only bring forth prophets, apostles, evangelists, pastors and teachers but shall also bring forth saviours" (Obadiah 1:21).

I wrote further, "Yet a little while and these saviours shall surface on the face of the whole earth. Joel 2, Zechariah 8 and all the related scriptures shall be fulfilled. The arrival of these saviours will compel the followership of multitudes that cannot be numbered. They will carry such aroma, the awesomeness of God will be so visible upon them, and their operations shall be unique and strange (We can see all these happening now). Yet a little while and saviours will surface on the face of the whole earth. Zion is in her month; this mighty army shall be released in just a moment."

Therefore, the essence of the new birth is once flesh, now spirit; once you were seated in the earthly realm, but now you have been raised up together with Christ Jesus and are now seated with Him in heavenly places. So you are a citizen of an entirely different Kingdom; your presence on earth is simply ambassadorial, and you are simply representing the interests of your place of origin.

> ***Now then we are ambassadors for Christ...***
>
> *2 Corinthians 5:20*

That means just as in the natural, ambassadors enjoy the immunities of the nations they represent. As an ambassador of Christ here on earth, you should enjoy all the immunities the Kingdom of God has to offer.

Also, ambassadors enjoy comfort proportional to the wealth of the country they represent. That is why embassy staff of certain nations move about in taxis while others have two cars attached to them. The poverty or wealth of the nations they represent naturally follows them wherever they go. New birth establishes a change in your citizenship, from earthly to the heavenly.

> ***And hath raised us up together, and made us sit together in heavenly places in Christ Jesus:***
>
> *Ephesians 2:6*

> ***He that cometh from above is above all: he that is of the earth is earthly, and speaketh of the earth: he that cometh from heaven is above all.***
>
> *John 3:31*

Chapter Four

The Purity Command

Nevertheless the foundation of God standeth sure, having this seal, The Lord knoweth them that are his. And, Let every one that nameth the name of Christ depart from iniquity.

If a man therefore purge himself from these, he shall be a vessel unto honour, sanctified, and meet for the master's use, and prepared unto every good work.

2 Timothy 2:19,21

Purity is the foundation of life in the supernatural. It guarantees an unending flow of miracles, signs and wonders in your life. Whenever purity is in place, miracles become the order of the day with you.

You have heard that signs and wonders are the heritage of all saints, but it takes power to produce signs, and this power will only flow through sanctified vessels. No purity, no power! Think about Gehazi, the servant of Elisha, he was destined to obtain a double portion of Elisha's anointing, but he lost it because sin was found in him!

A time came when Elisha gave Gehazi his rod to go and raise the dead son of the Shunammite woman (2 Kings 4), but the rod refused to answer. The reason was not very clear then, but it became evident later when Gehazi pursued Naaman for a talent of silver and two changes of garments. It was then the corruption in his heart was revealed. May corruption not be found in your heart!

Signs and wonders can never manifest in your life until corruption is dealt with. If the rod could not produce in Gehazi's hands, then it will not produce in the corrupt hands of any believer – no matter the kind of tongues you speak. Until sin goes, signs will not flow!
Jesus said:

> ***He that hath my commandments, and keepeth them, he it is that loveth me: and he that loveth me shall be loved of my Father, and I will love him, and will manifest myself to him.***
>
> *John 14:21*

"I will manifest myself to him" simply means, "I will bring him to the realm of supernatural manifestations if he will keep My commandment of purity." This implies that if you refuse to keep His commandment, you will automatically be disqualified for supernatural manifestations.

Jesus said, *Which of you convinceth me of sin?...* (John 8:46). What gave Him the boldness to ask such a question? He was a man of purity, a sanctified vessel, and as a result, He enjoyed supernatural manifestations throughout His life here on earth.

> ***Thou lovest righteousness, and hatest wickedness: therefore God, thy God, hath anointed thee with the oil of gladness above thy fellows.***
>
> ***All thy garments smell of myrrh, and aloes, and cassia, out of the ivory palaces, whereby they have made thee glad.***
>
> *Psalm 45:7-8*

The place of purity in the manifestations of signs and wonders cannot be overemphasised because it controls the release of the power you require to do signs (Mark 16:15-18). Therefore, if you are not a lover of purity, you cannot be a candidate for God's power.

The Virtues Of Purity

Among others, there are three powerful instruments that guarantee the flow of miracles, and all three are enhanced by purity. The first is:

Insight

> ***And he said unto them, Unto you it is given to know the mystery of the kingdom of God: but unto***

them that are without, all these things are done in parables:

Mark 4:11

The Kingdom of God is a Kingdom of mysteries. The scriptures make it clear that understanding these mysteries is your birthright as a saint: *...Unto you it is given to know the mystery of the kingdom of God...* But sin will block your access to those mysteries so that instead of understanding them, they remain parables to you. You become an outsider, and outsiders don't have access to inside stories; they are only for insiders. Who are those without?

For without are dogs, and sorcerers, and whoremongers, and murderers, and idolaters, and whosoever loveth and maketh a lie.

Revelation 22:15

Those without are dogs. But who are dogs?

But it is happened unto them according to the true proverb, The dog is turned to his own vomit again; and the sow that was washed to her wallowing in the mire.

2 Peter 2:22

Dogs are those who return to their vomit! They are the ones who say, "Lord, I am sorry" today but go back to their lying, cheating and adultery tomorrow. It is those people God considers "dog" Christians! Friend, you are a bonafide son of God, so you will not behave like a dog again because as long as you remain a "dog," you cannot gain access to the mysteries of God.

Think about this for a moment, no matter how much you love your dog, can it ever have access to certain information about you? For instance, does your dog know your bank account number or how much money you have in the bank? It is just not possible to confide such "inside stories" to your dog.

The Word is God's mystery bank; until you gain access to those mysteries, you never achieve mastery in life. Friend, information is no match for revelation. One is earthly, and the other is heavenly; one is of the mind, and the other is of the Spirit. And we know that:

> ***He that cometh from above is above all: he that is of the earth is earthly, and speaketh of the earth: he that cometh from heaven is above all.***
>
> *John 3:31*

Righteousness sets a pace for revelation; and revelation provokes revolutions! When you live in sin, you are limited to information from the Word of God; you never access revelations.

For instance, the miracles in Jesus' ministry could be attributed to the revelation He had from God. He said in John 5:19, 30:

> ***...Verily, verily, I say unto you, The Son can do nothing of himself, but what he seeth the Father do: for what things soever he doeth, these also doeth***

the Son likewise.

I can of mine own self do nothing: as I hear, I judge: and my judgment is just; because I seek not mine own will, but the will of the Father which hath sent me.

So the things He did were a function of the things He heard and saw. But He also had an outstanding testimony of purity (John 8:46). From today, you will also have an outstanding testimony of purity!

See what happens when you turn away from sin:

When I heard of the Signs and Wonders Week, I was prepared for it. But when I came for the service on Monday, I was in heavy pains, with boils in about five places all over my body.

When the Bishop said it was only holiness that would bring us close to God, I prayed (because he asked us to pray for forgiveness), then I asked for healing. I went home in pains and could not come to church on Tuesday.

I anointed myself, particularly the spots where the boils were, and by Wednesday morning, the boils had burst, and I am now relieved with all the pains gone. I return all the glory to God! — **Erhator S.**

For 12 years, I was held captive by the spirit of immorality. I gave my life to Christ in 1994, and when I read Proverbs 7:13-14, I began to cry, but this spirit still did not go. Then I made up my mind to wait on the Lord in the Word during the Signs and Wonders Week. Behold, I was totally delivered from the spirit of immorality!

Also, since 1990, I have been suffering from pile. It first came as haemorrhoids, and I took all sorts of drugs and native herbs; it subsided but resurfaced last year. While my anus was sticking out, I was drying up gradually. However, this week, I decided to wait on the Lord for my healing, and He healed me. Now, I am totally healed. I return all the glory to God! — **Adepoju O.**

For 15 years, I was addicted to marijuana. This started while I was in secondary school, and on several occasions, I had tried all to stop because my family was against it, but all efforts proved abortive. As such, it had stopped me from attaining my goals. However, in 1996, I joined this Commission; thereafter, I took a shot of the Anointing Oil, and that was the end of the 15 years bondage! Since then, good things have been manifesting in my life.

Meanwhile, I used to work in the bank, but I was relieved of my job. Thereafter, I set up my own company, an agro allied and food processing equipment company. Since I started worshipping here, things have been flourishing for me. I have been getting jobs worth 200,000 and one million naira. Recently, I was given a freelance marketing post in a newspaper house, which can fetch me about 50,000 naira monthly. I return all the glory to God! — **Sumonu K.**

> ***Turn you at my reproof: behold, I will pour out my spirit unto you, I will make known my words unto you.***
>
> *Proverbs 1:23*

I don't care how long you have been a victim of immorality, drug addiction or unforgiveness; if you will turn at His reproof, God will pour out His Spirit upon you and make His Words known to you, and you know that when the Word comes, you command the supernatural at will. That will be your portion from now on!

The Anointing

It is impossible to talk about signs and wonders without talking about the anointing. But as powerful as the anointing of the Holy Ghost is, it only produces for the consecrated; it only works for the pure.

> ***And he spake also a parable unto them; No man putteth a piece of a new garment upon an old; if otherwise, then both the new maketh a rent, and the piece that was taken out of the new agreeth not with the old.***
>
> ***And no man putteth new wine into old bottles; else the new wine will burst the bottles, and be spilled,***

and the bottles shall perish.

But new wine must be put into new bottles; and both are preserved.

Luke 5:36-38

When a man pours new wine into old wine skin, the old wine bottle breaks because the new wine is still fermenting and increasing in volume, but the old wine bottle has reached its elasticity limit. So, while the new wine in the old wine bottle keeps expanding, the wine bottle can expand no further, so it breaks, and both the bottle and wine are lost. That is why Jesus said that to preserve both wine and bottle, new wine must be put in a new wine bottle.

New wine represents the anointing of the Holy Spirit, and the wine bottle is the saints.

Others mocking said, These men are full of new wine.

For these are not drunken, as ye suppose, seeing it is but the third hour of the day.

But this is that which was spoken by the prophet Joel;

And on my servants and on my handmaidens I will pour out in those days of my Spirit; and they shall prophesy:

Acts 2:13,15-16,18

God cannot anoint you beyond your level of

consecration, or it may lead to your destruction. Since God is not a murderer, He must allow you attain a certain level of consecration before He anoints you.

Many pastors are just faking it all over town! A little lie here, a little adultery there until God washes His hands off them! So the pastor lays hands on people, and nothing happens, so with "boldface," he says, "It has happened; just give thanks." But there was no release of virtue, no unction because until purity is in place, he is not worthy of the new oil.

Divine Presence

The sea saw it, and fled: Jordan was driven back.

The mountains skipped like rams, and the little hills like lambs.

What ailed thee, O thou sea, that thou fleddest? thou Jordan, that thou wast driven back?

Ye mountains, that ye skipped like rams; and ye little hills, like lambs?

Tremble, thou earth, at the presence of the Lord, at the presence of the God of Jacob.

Psalm 114:3-7

The third virtue of purity is divine presence. Divine presence is the aura of God, His aroma and backing. When you carry God's presence, you compel the Jordans of life to be driven back; the seas of life see you and flee, the mountains skip like rams and the little hill like lambs. When the presence of God is with you, troubles bow to you; sickness merely hears the mention of your name and flees. Friend, the presence of God is worth any price you have to pay.

Talking of Jesus, Acts 10:38 says:

> ***How God anointed Jesus of Nazareth with the Holy Ghost and with power: who went about doing good, and healing all that were oppressed of the devil; for God was with him.***

The major secret of the signs and wonders in the ministry of Jesus was, *...For God was with him.* How did He attract God's presence?

> ***And he that sent me is with me: the Father hath not left me alone; for I do always those things that please him.***
>
> *John 8:29*

The miraculous did not answer to Jesus simply because He was the Son of God but because He did always the things that pleased the Father. God's presence is the master key to the supernatural.

What about the apostles? The Bible says:

> ***And they went forth, and preached everywhere, the Lord working with them, and confirming the word with signs following.***
>
> *Mark 16:20*

As long as the Lord was working with them, they commanded strange wonders wherever they went. Friend, the surest way to command the supernatural is to compel God's presence! Even apostle Paul, whom God used to do great wonders, was a carrier of the presence of God (Galatians 2:20).

God's presence is indispensable in your quest for the supernatural, but not without a price, and purity is the price that must be paid!

Jesus, the Son of God, never sinned; the apostles were men of rugged purity; apostle Paul was a man of integrity. These men were all reckoned with God as worthy vessels for His presence. Therefore, without purity, it is impossible to attract the presence of God.

Friend, just as Jesus and Paul were born to be signs to their generation, you are also born to be a sign. But if they could not carry the presence of God without purity, then purity is the all-important price to pay for divine presence. So, by all means, you must strive to stay pure.

> ***Who shall ascend into the hill of the Lord? or who shall stand in his holy place?***
>
> ***He that hath clean hands, and a pure heart; who hath not lifted up his soul unto vanity, nor sworn deceitfully.***
>
> ***He shall receive the blessing from the Lord, and righteousness from the God of his salvation.***
>
> *Psalm 24:3-5*

Chapter Five

The Word Command

It is the Word of God that makes you a commander of the supernatural. Therefore, no accomplishment is authentic, no miracle is genuine until it is founded upon the Word.

The name of Jesus is a potent force for the release of the supernatural; that is why Mark 16: 17 says, *And these signs shall follow them that believe; in my name shall they cast out devils...* But Psalm 138:2 tells us that despite of the potency of the name of Jesus, it cannot be compared with the Word in power.

> ***...For thou hast magnified thy word above all thy name.***

Therefore, the Word of God is God's number one instrument for producing miracles.

A young man came to me and said he needed a job.

I quoted Isaiah 3:10 to him, which says, *Say ye to the righteous, that it shall be well with him: for they shall eat the fruit of their doings.* Then I told him that the Bible said they shall eat the fruit of their doings, not the doings of their uncles or fathers. This means God has no plans for the righteous to be jobless. So I asked if he believed that, and he said he did, and I said to him, "Now, go and get a job!" He got a job the following week!

That miracle came by operating the Word. I did not need to pray; all I did was take charge of the situation by the Word.

It Is The Rod For Signs

> ***And thou shalt take this rod in thine hand, wherewith thou shalt do signs.***
>
> *Exodus 4:17*

God told Moses to take the rod in his hand and produce signs. That means the rod had the ability to command the miraculous. What or who is this rod?

> ***And there shall come forth a rod out of the stem of Jesse, and a Branch shall grow out of his roots:***
>
> ***And the spirit of the Lord shall rest upon him, the spirit of wisdom and understanding, the spirit of counsel and might, the spirit of knowledge and of the fear of the Lord;***
>
> *Isaiah 11:1-2*

The Lord's voice crieth unto the city, and the man of wisdom shall see thy name: hear ye the rod, and who hath appointed it.

Micah 6:9

Feed thy people with thy rod, the flock of thine heritage, which dwell solitarily in the wood, in the midst of Carmel: let them feed in Bashan and Gilead, as in the days of old.

Micah 7:14

So the rod is Jesus: He is the "rod out of the stem of Jesse," and He is the rod the Father has appointed. From an understanding of the scriptures, this same Jesus is also the Word of God (Revelation 19:13). Therefore, the rod is Jesus, and Jesus is the Word; so, the rod of signs is the Word of God!

Friend, it is with the Word of God you do signs. It is this Word that determines how much of the supernatural you experience in your life and actually shows you your worth in the world of the spirit.

For instance, I can confidently say I have a miracle home. How did I come about this miracle home? I discovered from the Word that *It is not good for man to be alone.* So I concluded that God must be saying, "I want to make life better (not worse) for him; let Me give him a wife." So marriage is not "for better for worse," but "for better for best!" God designed marriage for better.

Somewhere else, I read, *Two are better than one.* So I figured out that God has a better programme for me as a married man. Since I was not a fighter as a bachelor, I cannot be one when I am married.

Again, I discovered, *One shall chase a thousand and two shall put ten thousand to flight.* From this, I understood that I am designed for greater victory in life as a married man. Then I heard Him say in His Word, *...Be fruitful and multiply.* So I became convinced that fruitfulness in marriage is not a favour but part of the covenant pact God signed with man (Exodus 23:25-26).

All these are secrets discovered in the Word and things I have taken delivery of to ensure rest in my marital life. I can say with all boldness that my wife and I have not had the first argument in our home since we got married!

Nobody has the Word and lacks miracles. Every Word you encounter has the potential to produce a miracle for you.

Some time ago, Kenneth Hagin lay paralysed and dying on his sick bed. But then he encountered God's Word in Mark 11:23, which says:

> ***For verily I say unto you, That whosoever shall say unto this mountain, Be thou removed, and be thou cast into the sea; and shall not doubt in his heart, but shall believe that those things which he saith shall come to pass; he shall have whatsoever he saith.***

So he began to act on that Word. He would rise up and fall until he rose, never to fall again! That is the power in the Word at work! It cheaply delivers the miraculous into your hands.

> ***He sent his word, and healed them, and delivered them from their destructions.***
>
> *Psalm 107:20*

All that a man needs to do to provoke signs and wonders is, *Whatsoever he saith unto you, do it* (John 2:5). Until you do what He says, miracles are not in view. For instance, a businessman who knows what God says he should do and does it will have a flourishing business, the devil notwithstanding. In the same way, if a pastor knows what to do about his ministry and does it, he will succeed, no matter how many devils in hell are ganged up against him! That is why God laments at the ignorance of His people:

> ***My people are destroyed for lack of knowledge: because thou hast rejected knowledge, I will also reject thee, that thou shalt be no priest to me: seeing thou hast forgotten the law of thy God, I will also forget thy children.***
>
> *Hosea 4:6*

God's Word is the rod that commands the miraculous, and until you are in touch with the Word, you cannot be in touch with signs and wonders.

Some time ago, I encountered a powerful insight from

God's Word, which has resulted in diverse miracles in our ministry. I saw it in Genesis 2:7:

> ***And the Lord God formed man of the dust of the ground, and breathed into his nostrils the breath of life; and man became a living soul.***

I reasoned it must have been by the breath of God that clay took on life and blood began to flow in man. By this same breath, the muscles, tendons, etc., assumed their perfect positions. I couldn't imagine the internal organs being built separately by God and being put inside the figure He had formed. He formed man and His breath did the rest. When Jesus came, He exhibited the same kind of life the Father has:

> ***For as the Father hath life in himself; so hath he given to the Son to have life in himself;***
>
> ***And hath given him authority to execute judgment also, because he is the Son of man.***
>
> *John 5:26-27*

Not stopping there, I saw that redemption conferred on me the same quality of life Jesus and the Father have. Based on this scriptural analogy, I concluded that if the life in God, the Father, could create all the organs in the human body and also maintain them, then the eternal life in me carries creative and preservative power.

To validate this insight, I breathed into someone with the AIDS virus, and she was set free. On another occasion, a boy who was diagnosed with polio was healed after I breathed on his legs. Friend, signs and wonders result whenever you act on the Word. It always works!

On another occasion, as I sat meditating on the life of the three Hebrew boys in Babylon, I came to the place where it was written concerning them that they were ten times better than their colleagues. Then I saw from 2 Corinthians 3 that if the ministration of death is glorious, how much more glorious shall the ministration of righteousness be? So, I understood that redemption offers me a more glorious package than the law of Moses could have offered Shadrach, Meshach and Abednego.

Something began to tingle in my brain, and I found out that from that time, I could easily assimilate things to the point a one-time chief judge of a state asked where I got what he described as my "electric brain" from. You can collect a miracle mind from the pages of scripture!

In March 1981, I laid hold on the rod of prosperity and forced poverty out of my life. When I caught that insight, I proclaimed before men and devils, "I can never be poor!" At the time of this Word encounter, I had not been called into full-time ministry yet, so I was not reading to preach. But I was certain I had knocked the final nail into the coffin of poverty, and it died the same day.

Your business is not failing because there is a slump in your nation's economy but because there is a problem with your covenant walk! Nobody with the rod of prosperity can be enslaved by poverty. It is impossible! All you need do is set yourself to see the amazing things packaged in the Word for your liberation, and your destiny will be secured.

It is one thing to read, another to preach, and an entirely different thing to see, but only those who see possess their inheritance in God. So, set yourself to see mysteries from God's Word.

Jesus Himself did signs by what He heard and saw. Therefore, I can boldly say to you that everything contained in the Word is possible if only you set yourself to make discoveries. Stop pitying yourself or your situation; you don't have a special case. No matter how difficult that problem appears to be, there is a solution; all you need do is make scriptural discoveries.

Get To Know His Ways

> ***He made known his ways unto Moses, his acts unto the children of Israel.***
>
> *Psalm 103:7*

The ways of God are the highways to the miraculous. As soon as a man has an understanding of those ways, he becomes a commander of signs and wonders. Children may celebrate the acts of God (that accounts for the cheers when a miracle is performed), but mature believers are in touch with the ways of the Almighty. His ways decide the acts, so His ways are superior to the acts.

That is what made Moses a General in the Kingdom of God. Despite his experiences with God, he still yearned to know His ways more.

> ***Now therefore, I pray thee, if I have found grace in thy sight, show me now thy way, that I may know thee, that I may find grace in thy sight: and consider that this nation is thy people.***
>
> *Exodus 33:13*

Jesus needed to feed 5,000 men, besides women and children, who are generally more in number at crusades. The Bible says concerning Him:

> ***And this he said to prove him: for he himself knew what he would do.***
>
> *John 6:6*

The knowledge of God's ways produced the miracle food that fed the entire lot. Jesus had an understanding that compelled the flow of signs.

I remember announcing to a gathering of people at the outset of the ministry that God told me not to look up to them. He said, "You have two eyes; can you make one eye to look up and the other to look down?" I tried and could not, then God said, "Anytime you are looking unto men, never claim to be looking unto Me. For they that look unto Me are lightened, and their faces are not ashamed."

I must have found something that made me speak as I did. I understood my assignment from the pages of the scriptures. I understood God's covenant pact, so I did not have any fear as to whether it would work or not; I was so sure it would. As you go for the ways of God, I see you walk on the highways of life.

The Word Makes You A god!

> ***Jesus answered them, Is it not written in your law, I said, Ye are gods?***
>
> ***If he called them gods, unto whom the word of God came, and the scripture cannot be broken;***
>
> ***Say ye of him, whom the Father hath sanctified, and sent into the world, Thou blasphemest; because I said, I am the Son of God?***
>
> *John 10:34-36*

The above scripture implies that when the Word of God enters your heart on any particular subject of life, it automatically makes you a god over that circumstance and causes you to operate in the realm of the gods – the supernatural.

Being a walking Bible who can reel off any number of memory verses is no proof that the word has gained access to you.

Those He called gods are those unto whom the Word of God came. It is the incoming (the entrance) of the Word to a man that affects a change in his status. It is the entrance, not the reading or preaching or the confession, but the entrance of the Word. When the Word of God comes into you on any issue confronting you, light has come, and darkness must flee.

Your Access To The Word

> ***My son, eat thou honey, because it is good; and the honeycomb, which is sweet to thy taste:***
>
> ***So shall the knowledge of wisdom be unto thy soul: when thou hast found it, then there shall be a reward, and thy expectation shall not be cut off.***
>
> *Proverbs 24:13-14*

The answers to the questions of life are available in the Book, but no one finds the answer without knowing. It is he that seeketh that findeth. Friend, you cannot find the Word and not know, *...When thou hast found it, then there shall be a reward, and thy expectation shall not be cut off.*

There is a search required, but if you are not ready to search, you will be too smart to find. There is no guesswork in this matter (that makes for certainty), but you must be willing to pay the price to get at knowledge.

Meditation

To meditate means to consider deeply, reflect upon or revolve in the mind. It is similar to the physical process of food digestion. When you eat food, it undergoes three major processes before the nutrients in it can benefit the body. They are: digestion, absorption and assimilation.

Many times, we think the taste of food in the mouth and its weight in the stomach is all there is to food. But until these three processes take place, the food you eat adds no value to the body. No matter how delicious what you eat is, it must be broken down into 'assimilable' forms so that your body can absorb the nutrients in it.

Similarly, until the Word of God you hear or read is broken down into 'assimilable' forms, and you contact the gems in it, your life cannot be bettered by it. The meditation process breaks down the Word into digestible forms, equipping you to walk on the highways of the miraculous.

> ***Thy words were found, and I did eat them; and thy word was unto me the joy and rejoicing of mine heart: for I am called by thy name, O Lord God of hosts.***
>
> *Jeremiah 15:16*

The time many people spend in prayers should actually be dedicated to meditation. In times of difficulty, you hear people ask, "Have you prayed through?" But no one asks, "Have you thought through?" But solutions come easily as you settle down to think through the scriptures. The best of the covenant is accessible only to successful "meditators."

> ***This book of the law shall not depart out of thy mouth; but thou shalt meditate therein day and night, that thou mayest observe to do according to all that is written therein: for then thou shalt make thy way prosperous, and then thou shalt have good success.***
>
> *Joshua 1:8*

But the Church is so tied to the old syllabus that it keeps suffering the same age-old plagues and difficulties. God has made His Word available as an instrument for combating life's woes. But the power in the Word is only released through the process of meditation. Until you ponder on the truth contained in the Word, get an understanding of that Word and act on it, you cannot display miracles, signs and wonders.

Through meditation, you can cheaply collect effective strategies for success in your business, family, career, etc. While you are before the Lord in your quiet time, ponder on the Word of God concerning any area of difficulty in your life. Tell yourself, "This thing ought not to be, so how do I resolve it?"

As you wait before the Lord, light will begin to flood your heart, showing you practical solutions to the negative situations of life.

Some time ago, I heard a voice within me say, "Who says the devil is not powerful?" At the same instance, floods of negative thoughts came rushing through my mind. I remembered certain negative things that had occurred in my extended family and which would have made me afraid, except that as suddenly as the evil wind blew, three scriptures came to my mind annulling the effect of those words. The first was Romans 13:1-2:

> ***Let every soul be subject unto the higher powers. For there is no power but of God: the powers that be are ordained of God.***
>
> ***Whosoever therefore resisteth the power, resisteth the ordinance of God: and they that resist shall receive to themselves damnation.***

So I reasoned that God would not institute any power against Himself because a kingdom divided against itself cannot stand.

Then I also saw that in Matthew 28:18, Jesus said:

> ***...All power is given unto me in heaven and in earth.***

Finally, the Psalmist said:

> ***God hath spoken once; twice have I heard this; that power belongeth unto God.***
>
> *Psalm 62:11*

So, I reacted rudely against Satan on the basis of these Words, exercising my authority over him, and he left me alone! Satan will leave you alone!

Meditation brings you into encounters with the intoxicating Word of God. That is why it is not a question of how many chapters of the Bible you read in a day that determines your ability to flow in signs and wonders but the quantity you successfully assimilate.

Sometime ago, while meditating on John 1, I saw how cheaply one can destroy the stronghold of darkness with light. I discovered there is no contesting the supremacy of light in any conflict against darkness. I discovered the power of light.

Shortly after, I went to my hometown for Christmas and was told one of my cousins had been afflicted with insanity. When I learnt this, I was excited because I saw an opportunity to manifest the truth of the Word I had just encountered.

So I went to the room he was in, and as soon as I entered, he prostrated to greet me; he could recognise me in his madness! I asked his brothers to put him in my car, saying, "Let me see the devil that will follow him into my car." We had scarcely driven a few kilometres when this cousin of mine fell sound asleep (he had not slept in days)!

When he was taken to the teaching hospital the following day, he was asked, "What is wrong with you?" But he replied, "Do you mean what was wrong with me or what is wrong with me?" The doctors needed no further proof that he was healed! The same young man has since graduated from the university; he is working and married with kids!

> ***And the light shineth in darkness; and the darkness comprehended it not.***
>
> *John 1:5*

May God make you a successful "meditator" of His Word!

Quietness

> ***...Study to be quiet...***
>
> *1 Thessalonians 4:11*

> ***For the Egyptians shall help in vain, and to no purpose: therefore have I cried concerning this, Their strength is to sit still.***
>
> ***For thus saith the Lord God, the Holy One of Israel; In returning and rest shall ye be saved; in quietness and in confidence shall be your strength: and ye would not.***
>
> ***But ye said, No; for we will flee upon horses; therefore shall ye flee: and, We will ride upon the swift; therefore shall they that pursue you be swift.***
>
> *Isaiah 30:7,15-16*

One other avenue through which you can receive insight from the Word of God is quietness. It is a remarkable strategy for accessing revelations to bring revolutions in your life.

God came to Adam at the cool of the day, when everywhere was calm and serene. So God still comes visiting when everywhere is calm.

It is in the "cool" of the day you often encounter insight or light from God's Word. At such times, as you begin to ponder on certain scriptures, solutions to situations are handed over to you. It is also at such times of quietness every weak area of your life is strengthened.

> ***For the people shall dwell in Zion at Jerusalem: thou shalt weep no more: he will be very gracious unto thee at the voice of thy cry; when he shall hear it, he will answer thee.***
>
> ***And though the Lord give you the bread of adversity, and the water of affliction, yet shall not thy teachers be removed into a corner any more, but thine eyes shall see thy teachers:***
>
> ***And thine ears shall hear a word behind thee, saying, This is the way, walk ye in it, when ye turn to the right hand, and when ye turn to the left.***
>
> *Isaiah 30:19-21*

God is saying in this scripture that He will raise teachers who will instruct you. So when you are quiet on the inside, your spiritual ear will hear a voice behind you saying, "This is the way; walk in it." Such teachers are in the form of books or tapes, so as you follow their messages, God causes your ear to hear a word. It may not come directly from the teaching but from the Lord showing you what to do concerning that issue.

That was how I contacted the secrets of Kingdom prosperity. I went to a quiet place armed with *The Law of Prosperity*, written by Kenneth Copeland, *God's Will Is Prosperity*, by Gloria Copeland (his wife), and my Bible. I was in that quiet place for three days. I programmed quietness for myself, and as I read the books and the Bible, I found what I was looking for.

The secret I located was not in either of the books; it came as I read my Bible. I got to where I saw the infallibility of God's covenant, and I knew I could never be a bedmate with poverty again!

I pity men and women who claim to be too busy to settle down to locate where next to go or what next to do from the Word. Please note that there is no substitute for light in the conflict against darkness. Therefore, create an atmosphere of quietness for God's visitation, and it will end all your life's struggles.

Understanding

The Ethiopian eunuch in Acts 8 was reading from Isaiah 53 but did not understand what he was reading until Philip, moved by the Holy Ghost, asked him, *Understandest thou what thou readest?* Philip opened him up to the benefits of that scripture.

Until you understand any scripture, the benefits

are not released to you. It is your understanding that connects you to the virtues in the Word. Once understanding comes, miracles are inevitable.

Understanding begets faith. That was why as soon as the Ethiopian eunuch understood what Philip was saying, he said, "See, here is water; what doth hinder me to be baptized?"

Once you have the Word, you have access to the miraculous. All you need to do is lay hold on it and operate with it. You can live free from sickness, family crises, financial troubles, etc., if you encounter light from the Word. Nothing gets God committed to act on your behalf as His Word, so go for it.

It is time to sit up and say, "Lord, I know that if I can lay hold on the Word, I will command signs and wonders." Remember that everything is under the control of the Word, so an encounter with the Word puts you perfectly in command of the situations of life.

Chapter Six

The Faith Command

Jesus said unto him, If thou canst believe, all things are possible to him that believeth.

Mark 9:23

Many people have thought that when it comes to the subject of miracles, man has no part to play because it is entirely up to God. But that is not true. Miracles are not accidental occurrences; they are the deliberate acts of God, provoked by the desperate faith of men. That means, as far as God is concerned, miracles are provoked by the die-hard faith of man.

When men come to their wits' end, they say, "It will take a miracle." As soon as you hear that, you conclude they mean, "It will only take God" because everybody knows that when it comes to the question of miracles, only God has the answer!

God is a miracle worker! That is His job. In fact, miracles are as natural to Him as eating is to man. Whereas man is surprised when miracles occur, God, on the other hand, is surprised when miracles do not occur. But God will only act when He sees faith. Faith is the connection between man and the miracle-working power of God.

Please get this straight: God is a miracle worker; that is His job. He does not deny Himself; He abides faithful; He is not a whimsical God who does things haphazardly! He is constant and unchanging. But the main issue is man. God's side is intact; man is the only variable. Today, he believes, and tomorrow, he walks in doubt and unbelief. But God will not move on your behalf until Faith is involved.

The Work of Faith

When the Jews observed how miracles cheaply answered to Jesus, they asked:

> ***... What shall we do, that we might work the works of God?***
>
> *John 6:28*

And Jesus said:

> ***...This is the work of God, that ye believe on him whom he hath sent.***
>
> *John 6:29*

Therefore, the cardinal way to *work the works of God* is by faith. I am not talking about the mental assent of "I believe" but the "work" known as faith. You may ask, "Is faith a work?" Hear this:

> ***Verily, verily, I say unto you, He that believeth on me, the works that I do shall he do also; and greater works than these shall he do; because I go unto my Father.***
>
> *John 14:12*

Faith Is Work!

Consider the account of the woman with the issue of blood: while many people were thronging Jesus, she was pressing through by faith to touch Jesus and draw virtue for the healing of her body. That was not just the mental assent of "I believe Jesus can heal me." The multitude believed, but she connected to signs and wonders by her faith. That is the work of faith! Jesus crowned it all by saying:

> ***...Daughter, thy faith hath made thee whole; go in peace, and be whole of thy plague.***
>
> *Mark 5:34*

Friend, without faith, you cannot do signs, and you cannot receive signs. Without faith, you are sign-barren! Therefore, you need the instrument of faith to work miracles.

> ***And when Jesus departed thence, two blind men followed him, crying, and saying, Thou son of***

David, have mercy on us.

And when he was come into the house, the blind men came to him: and Jesus saith unto them, Believe ye that I am able to do this? They said unto him, Yea, Lord.

Then touched he their eyes, saying, According to your faith be it unto you.

Matthew 9:27-29

The tears of the blind men did not move Jesus to act on their behalf. So, tears do not produce miracles. It is sad to see many still crying after Jesus for miracles in the Church today. They have been following for long, crying after Him for signs and wonders. Some fast for 40, 70 and even 100 days, just crying for miracles, but weeping will not produce signs!

The same question Jesus asked the blind men is the same question He is still asking people today: *Believe ye that I am able to do this?* Until faith is in place, your tears are a waste. How long you have been following Him is irrelevant; what will deliver the sign into your hand is your faith. For without faith, it is impossible to please God (Hebrews 11:6).

In Acts 14:8-10, the story is told of a man who had been lame from his mother's womb. He received his miracle simply on the platform of faith. As a matter of fact, nobody picked him up; he rose up by himself! As he arose, strength came to his lame legs. Paul, looking at him perceived, he had faith to be healed. Faith is what connects you to the miraculous.

I discovered that in Hebrews 11, all the men mentioned there were men of faith. For instance, Enoch was translated and did not see death because of his faith. Moses' amazing ministry was run and sustained largely by faith.

> **By faith *Moses, when he was born, was hid three months of his parents, because they saw he was a proper child; and they were not afraid of the king's commandment.***
>
> **By faith *Moses, when he was come to years, refused to be called the son of Pharaoh's daughter...***
>
> **By faith *he forsook Egypt, not fearing the wrath of the king: for he endured, as seeing him who is invisible.***
>
> **Through faith *he kept the passover, and the sprinkling of blood, lest he that destroyed the firstborn should touch them.***
>
> ***By faith they passed through the Red sea as by dry land: which the Egyptians assaying to do were drowned.***
>
> *Hebrews 11:23-29*

That enormous ministry, characterised by mind-boggling wonders, was a product of faith! I paraphrased Hebrews 11:6 to read:

> ***But without faith it is impossible to move God; for***

he that cometh to God must believe that He is, and is up to the task he's presenting before Him.

The Force of Faith

> ***Now faith is the substance of things hoped for, the evidence of things not seen.***
>
> *Hebrews11:1*

Faith is a substance; it is not a figment of man's imagination, and neither is it a psychological state of mind. Faith is a substance; it is a tangible, "takeable," and "handleable" force. If it is not a substance, you cannot take it.

> ***Above all,* taking the shield of faith, *wherewith ye shall be able to quench all the fiery darts of the wicked.***
>
> *Ephesians 6:16*

Faith is a living force drawn from the living Word to produce living proofs. It is the trigger that provokes supernatural interventions. It is beyond the mental sphere and not a physical force; it is a spiritual entity. How then do we take delivery of it?

> ***So then faith cometh by hearing, and hearing by the word of God.***
>
> *Romans 10:17*

The Word of God is the delivery van of faith; it transports faith to you. The Word can also be likened to a pregnant woman and the child in the womb faith. Only those who labour in the Word deliver faith. Just as a pregnant woman must go into labour before her child is born, you must labour in the Word of God before faith can be born.

Friend, you cannot have faith without knowing, just as a child cannot be born without the mother's knowledge. Which mother can forget the labour that precedes the birth of her child? Faith does not come in the labour ward but in the "Labour Word." As you labour in the Word, you will take delivery of your miracle in Jesus' name!

One woman was prepared to labour in the Word until she took delivery of her miracle baby.

Three months before my wedding, I stopped menstruating. After my wedding, I went to see the doctor, and the first he said was, 'Madam, I am sorry you will find it difficult to take in'. The second one said, 'Sorry, without menstruating, ovulation cannot take place. Without ovulation, you cannot get pregnant'. Then he said, 'Tell your husband to get about 10,000 to 100,000 naira ready, and I will carry out different tests to know what exactly is wrong with you'.

Initially, I ran from one hospital to another, seeing different gynaecologists. Later, I got hold of one of Bishop's books titled ***You Shall Not Be Barren!*** *The first paragraph I read said, 'There is no biological reason strong enough to hold married couples from getting pregnant if they* *want to'. I held on to that. He further said, 'The Bible says, be fruitful and multiply.' Then I said to myself, 'Menses or no menses, I am getting pregnant!'*

During the last Feet-washing Service in 1996, I came here and was seated under the canopy. The Bishop said, 'Today, the devil will see you and cry'. I said amen. Again, He said, 'Today, we are going to disgrace the devil and give God a serious dance'. So he called on the song leader to lead us in worshipping God in the Ijesha dialect. The talking drum was playing full swing, and I began to dance.

When it was my turn to wash my feet, I dipped them inside the water and said enough of barrenness, enough of unfruitfulness. Today, menses or no menses, I would have my baby. I would come with my baby to the last Feet-washing service in 1997. After my feet were washed, I danced as if I was out in a competition.

My husband was not at the service, so when I got home, I said to him, 'Look, our baby is ready', and he said, 'Okay'. In January, I went to the hospital to see my doctor; I told him I was pregnant, and he said, 'Okay, let us carry out the most accurate test, which is the blood pregnancy test'. When the result came back, it was negative. I went home and told my husband, and he said the doctor did not see well.

In February, I went back to the hospital and told my doctor to examine me because I was pregnant. He said,

'Madam, I don't mean to frighten you. I don't think you can be pregnant. I am sure it is because of your menstrual cycle. It is either you have PID (Pelvic Inflammatory Disease), ectopic pregnancy or the ovarian cyst is still disturbing you'.

But I told the doctor I don't have any of those diseases. Then he said, 'Why are you so sure?' and I said it is because from Genesis to Revelation, there was nothing like that. So he asked me to do a scan again.

By the time I got to the scan doctor's door, I began to shake. He saw me and said, 'But woman, I have scanned you before'. Then I told God not to make me a case study in this hospital. The man placed his scanning machine on me and said, 'Woman, you are pregnant!' And I began to cry. So I asked him how many months the pregnancy was, and he said 11 weeks and four days. Today, I have my baby in my hands; a bouncing baby boy. I return all the glory to God! — **Olowosuko A.**

Faith Gives Substance To Hope

When the Bible talks about faith being the substance of things hoped for, it means the things you hope for or expect cannot be realised until you inject faith into them. It is faith plus hope that equals manifestation.

Many people miss it by hoping for miracles without activating their faith. But hope alone is nothing but an idle wish. It is faith that makes it a reality. For example,

I cannot see me fail; that is my expectation, my hope. But to give it substance, I have to locate God's Word that guarantees that success will answer to me.

Faith Guarantees Rest

> ***For we which have believed do enter into rest, as he said, As I have sworn in my wrath, if they shall enter into my rest: although the works were finished from the foundation of the world.***
>
> *Hebrews 4:3*

Can you imagine a family without problems, a ministry without crises, a body without sickness, a pocket that is never empty, and a life without worries? Nothing defines the word "rest" more than these.

Rest is a worry-free existence. It is a much sought-after commodity because nobody wants to live in worry. However, the sure access to God's rest is faith.

> ***There remaineth therefore a rest to the people of God.***
>
> ***For he that is entered into his rest, he also hath ceased from his own works, as God did from his.***
>
> ***Let us labour therefore to enter into that rest, lest any man fall after the same example of unbelief.***
>
> *Hebrews 4:9-11*

It is labouring in the Word of God that guarantees rest. You stay at the Word until you encounter faith, which leads to rest. It was tedious to go for three days in search of prosperity, but I stayed at the Word until faith came, and its result was financial rest. Having laboured, I have "ceased from my own works," as God ceased from His. Abundance now attends to me naturally. There is no other way to live in the miraculous outside faith, and it is those who labour in the Word that encounters it.

I like the word "labour." Jesus said to the multitudes:

> ***... Verily, verily, I say unto you, Ye seek me, not because ye saw the miracles, but because ye did eat of the loaves, and were filled.***
>
> ***Labour not for the meat which perisheth, but for that meat which endureth unto everlasting life, which the Son of man shall give unto you: for him hath God the Father sealed.***
>
> *John 6:26-27*

Jesus was telling them not to labour for perishable bread but for the Bread of life — the Word of God because the bread of life produces the faith, which establishes us in His rest. The moment faith comes, rest has come. *If thou canst believe, all things are possible to him that believeth.* When all things become possible to you, your rest is established.

That is why you cannot afford to be Word weary. As long as you keep hungering for the Word, you are on the path to the miraculous. I am not talking about just reading, but reading, searching, and meditating until faith strikes in your heart. The moment faith strikes, there is a sigh of relief because rest has come.

> ***Let us labour therefore to enter into that rest, lest any man fall after the same example of unbelief.***
>
> ***For the word of God is quick, and powerful, and sharper than any two-edged sword, piercing even to the dividing asunder of soul and spirit, and of the joints and marrow, and is a discerner of the thoughts and intents of the heart.***
>
> *Hebrews 4:11-12*

I love Doddie Osteen's testimony. She was struck with terminal cancer, and her husband, a mighty man of God, had prayed for her, but borrowing Bible words, *She was nothing bettered.* He invited other mighty men of God, who also prayed, but there was still no improvement.

With just six more days to live, Doddie settled down with the Word and located forty powerful scriptures that guaranteed victory over cancer and death. With the last strength she had left in her, she began to feed on these scriptures until faith struck in her heart. In other words, she sat down and mixed those 40 scriptures with faith in the laboratory of her heart. Several years after her appointed day of death, she is still hale and hearty today!

> ***For unto us was the gospel preached, as well as unto them: but the word preached did not profit them,***

not being mixed with faith in them that heard it.
Hebrews 4:2

Some years ago, I wrote a book titled *Power Over Death*. The title scared a lot of people, so I retitled it *Long Life Your Heritage.* That book came from a weeklong seminar on the weakness of death over the believer. But first, I had sat down with scriptures, running through Genesis to Revelation until I discovered that death does not have the final say in the life of a child of God.

Shortly after my discoveries, death literally came to my room. I was at the point of death when the Holy Spirit on my inside asked me, "What are you doing here?" And I replied, "I don't know too." With that, I jumped out of bed, went to the bathroom, got dressed and went on a journey, saying, "Any death on my way, I will drive over your head and break you." That was not just a boast but a statement rooted in the light I had just received from God's Word.

When God's Word is ignited by faith in your heart, you command signs and wonders. But without faith, it is impossible to provoke miracles.

At a time, death came to take our last daughter and was actually taking her away. But I went into my office, locked the door and said to myself, "There is always a way out of any situation. I am here to locate that way." I laboured in the quick and powerful Word of God until I found certain nuggets that forbade the activity of death over my offspring. I squeezed out the substance in them until faith rose up in me and gave me the authority required for victory.

At that point, I knew death had lost the battle. When she recovered, I wrote a poem welcoming her back. I wrote, "She had been in a basket, as it were, on the waters of death, but the crocodiles could not eat her." All through the period she was down, there was no crying, vibrating or gyrating from me. I simply laboured in the Word until faith came and death was swallowed up in victory!

There is no point waiting for miracles to happen on their own accord; you can make them happen! A choice to wait is a choice to waste. Don't say, "I know someday I will be pregnant." If you are barren, today can be that day for you. Many people have waited like that for years without getting anything in the end.

But your miracle is available today! What you really need is the key to faith. Once it comes, your mountains will be levelled, and the impossible will become possible.

Therefore faith is the cheapest way to continuous victory (1 John 5:4). It is also the ticket to life in the miraculous. Once you are born of God, faith is your emblem; it is your staff of office and authority in the midst of conflict.

Chapter Seven

The Spirit Command

But ye shall receive power, after that the Holy Ghost is come upon you: and ye shall be witnesses unto me both in Jerusalem, and in all Judaea, and in Samaria, and unto the uttermost part of the earth.
Acts 1:8

The Holy Spirit is the producer of miracles on the earth today. That means although you are, by redemption, a miracle worker, your identity never becomes a reality until the Holy Ghost comes upon you. So it is impossible to separate signs from the operation of the Spirit of God.

The man Moses was a man mightily used by God to do many wonders in Egypt, and the Bible reveals his secret:

And I will come down and talk with thee there: and I will take of the spirit which is upon thee, and will

> ***put it upon them; and they shall bear the burden of the people with thee, that thou bear it not thyself alone.***
>
> *Numbers 11:17*

The Spirit of God was at work in him. Therefore, it was the Holy Spirit who worked through Moses.

What about Jesus, the New Testament Moses? As a young Jewish boy, He must have attended the synagogue faithfully; He was dedicated, yet, not distinguished. It was not until He returned to Galilee in the power of the Spirit the miraculous began to find expression through Him.

> ***And Jesus returned in the power of the Spirit into Galilee: and there went out a fame of him through all the region round about.***
>
> *Luke 4:14*

What about the disciples? They were timidly and cowardly hiding away in the upper room after Jesus Christ ascended into heaven. But on the day of Pentecost, the Holy Ghost descended upon them, and their ministry exploded! The coming of the Holy Spirit launched them into realms of "notable" miracles. He brought them out of hiding into the limelight. When they healed the lame man at the Beautiful Gate, the world took knowledge of them that they had been with Jesus.

As a Christian, you cannot become a sign until the Holy Spirit comes upon you. As it were, you remain in hiding in your business, ministry, career, etc., until the Holy Ghost comes. But when He comes upon you, you begin to experience profiting in every area of life.

> ***But the manifestation of the Spirit is given to every man to profit withal.***
>
> *1 Corinthians 12:7*

Measures Of The Spirit

> ***And when the man that had the line in his hand went forth eastward, he measured a thousand cubits, and he brought me through the waters; the waters were to the ankles.***
>
> ***Again he measured a thousand, and brought me through the waters; the waters were to the knees. Again he measured a thousand, and brought me through; the waters were to the loins.***
>
> ***Afterward he measured a thousand; and it was a river that I could not pass over: for the waters were risen, waters to swim in, a river that could not be passed over.***
>
> *Ezekiel 47:3-5*

The Holy Spirit is given to us in measures. At new birth, it is impossible to say, "Jesus is Lord" without the conviction of the Holy Spirit (1 Corinthians 12:3). Once you are born-again, you are qualified for the next phase, which is the baptism of the Holy Spirit.

On the day of Pentecost, when the people asked, *Men*

and brethren, what shall we do? Peter replied, *Repent, and be baptized every one of you in the name of Jesus Christ for the remission of sins, and ye shall receive the gift of the Holy Ghost* (Acts 2:37-38). There is a baptism that follows repentance.

When I gave my life to Christ (I was led to Christ by an Evangelical), I was told I was complete in Christ and did not require the baptism of the Holy Spirit. I agreed with all I was told, so I suffered along with them.

However, while praying one day, I found myself saying, "Holy Spirit, if You are anywhere, come to me now because I am not sure of this thing," and I was filled with the Holy Ghost. I spoke a strange language, yet, it was very refreshing, and I knew it had to be from God because the devil does not bring comfort to anybody. So many great men are still locked up in that doctrine today; as a result, remain practically powerless.

The next measure of the Spirit is the anointing. It is the divine enabling of the Holy Spirit. Jesus, although born of the Spirit, could not manifest His glory until He was anointed with the Holy Spirit. He was known as the carpenter's son for 30 years without any outstanding accomplishments until the anointing came. The Holy Spirit is the fountain for the miraculous.

That was why Jesus could not get started in ministry until He was anointed by the Spirit. But when the anointing came, He was in a crowd someday and asked,

Who touched me? Peter said, "Master, the multitude throng thee and press thee, and sayest thou, Who touched me?" But Jesus said, *Somebody hath touched me: for I perceive that virtue is gone out of me* (Luke 8:45-46).

That virtue Jesus talked about also means unction. In other words, virtue went out of Him to effect a sign somewhere. Once there is a flow of unction, there is bound to be a manifestation of signs and wonders.

The apostles could not break forth into the realm of the miraculous until they were first filled with the Holy Spirit on the day of Pentecost. As a result of that infilling, they healed a lame man at the Beautiful Gate in chapter three. In chapter four, they desired an increase in the measure of the Spirit upon their lives, so they prayed:

> ***...And grant unto thy servants, that with all boldness they may speak thy word,***
>
> ***By stretching forth thine hand to heal; and that signs and wonders may be done by the name of thy holy child Jesus.***
>
> ***And when they had prayed, the place was shaken where they were assembled together; and they were all filled with the Holy Ghost, and they spake the word of God with boldness.***
>
> *Acts 4:29-31*

The result of that prayer is recorded in chapter 5:12:

And by the hands of the apostles were many signs and wonders wrought among the people; and they were all with one accord in Solomon's porch.

The result of the anointing of the Holy Ghost upon their lives was an explosion of signs and wonders! But there is another realm and measure of the Spirit. Jesus revealed it when He said:

Verily, verily, I say unto you, He that believeth on me, the works that I do shall he do also; and greater works than these shall he do; because I go unto my Father.

John 14:12

But how shall we do greater works than He did except we have access to the source of signs as He had. Jesus had the anointing of the Holy Spirit without measure, and that accounted for His unique ministry (John 3:34). If we are to do the works He did, and greater, it means we must have access to the immeasurable anointing He had.

Ezekiel 47:3-5 paints a graphic picture of the anointing of the Holy Spirit. Verse five describes the immeasurable realm of the anointing:

Afterward he measured a thousand; and it was a river that I could not pass over: for the waters were risen, waters to swim in, a river that could not be passed over.

You also have access to the anointing of the Holy Spirit

without measure. When you have this understanding, you will find yourself working signs at will.

On my way to the church auditorium one day, a man, who had sustained spinal injuries in a motor accident and was wearing a lumber jacket, touched the flowing gown I had on and was healed.

Another woman could not defecate without medical assistance. However, she came to the *Healing School* one day. So I left my coat, instructing anybody looking up to God for healing to touch it. This woman touched the jacket and felt something loosen inside her. Immediately, she went to the toilet. For the first time in 38 years, she could defecate by herself!

These manifestations are not gimmicks to bring people to church. No, they are divine proofs of the flow of virtue.

Friend, the manifestation of the Spirit is your ticket to commanding the supernatural. This is why you must desperately desire an increase in the measure of the Spirit upon your life because the greater your measure, the greater the degree of your manifestation.

Your Access To The Spirit

> ***Turn you at my reproof: behold, I will pour out my spirit unto you, I will make known my words unto you.***
>
> *Proverbs 1:23*

The principal access to the anointing of the Holy Spirit is **purity**. God will not anoint you beyond your level of purity because it could spell your destruction. That is why until a man turns at the reproof of the Lord, it is never his turn to enjoy an increase in unction. Does anyone put new wine into old wine bottles? No! This is because the bottle will burst, and the new wine will be a waste (Luke 5:37).

Jesus, who was anointed without measure, got to that level because He knew no sin. The unction upon Him was a function of His consecration (Psalm 45:7). Apostle Paul was a man of a strange order of signs, and he was also the most outspoken apostle against sin.

> ***Ye are witnesses, and God also, how holily and justly and unblameably we behaved ourselves among you that believe:***
>
> *1 Thessalonians 2:10*

Until your love for righteousness increases, your level of unction can never increase. Going on a 40-day fast is not a substitute for purity, and neither is crying and weeping for the anointing. It is your consecration that determines how far you go in God. Do you want to live a life of signs and wonders? Then you must be prepared to step out of sin. I am not just talking about obvious sins like adultery, but hidden sins as well; sins of the heart, a filthy mind, etc.

Friend, you are the initiator of every change in your

life. You can leave the ordinary realm to the miraculous if you embrace this word of righteousness. Until righteousness is in place, you will never have an increase in anointing. The Holy Spirit wants to come to you, but He is not permitted to come into dirty vessels. When you consecrate yourself, then are you set to receive Him.

Remember Ezekiel 47? I believe the Holy Spirit takes a man to the level his consecration allows. If He takes you to the ankle deep, and you clean up some more, He will take you to the knee level. If He observes that you have cleaned up a little more, He will take you to the loin level and on to the river level. You must get there!

Chapter Eight

The Sound Command

Mere knowledge of the supernatural world won't bring about its manifestation. You need an understanding of the dynamics of its operations if you must benefit from it. A cardinal step in the release of the supernatural is the production of sound. The production of sound based on the Word of God revealed to you will compel supernatural forces to work in your favour. That is what brings about the signs you desire.

Therefore, soundless Christians are signless Christians. The night discussion between Jesus and Nicodemus is very revealing of the dynamics of sound production.

> ***The wind bloweth where it listeth, and thou hearest the sound thereof, but canst not tell whence it cometh, and whither it goeth: so is every one that is born of the Spirit.***
>
> *John 3:8*

When the wind blows, and you hear the sound distinctly, it is evident that the wind is blowing. In the same way, everyone that is born of the Spirit produces sounds. You must be heard for the supernatural to be released in your life. Everyone born of the Spirit of God is designed for sound production. This is the switch that sets the supernatural in motion. Just like no one understands the movement of the wind, the sound of the believers may not be understood. Yes, you hear the sound, but you may never understand it until you see the effect.

Get this straight; your mouth is a weapon of authority ordained by God to keep you in perfect dominion. It is your instrument for the exercise of supernatural authority. Jesus said everyone that is born of the Spirit is like the wind. You must make distinct sounds with your mouth concerning what you desire before you can see a sign in that direction.

Every sign and wonder is a direct product of a sound. That is why only the confident loudmouths command the miraculous in the Kingdom. Many people in church are too religious to manifest signs and wonders. They keep a closed mouth and a complaining heart. If you say positive things based on the word of God in your heart, you will get positive results. The same is true for negative words. As a believer, the basis of whatever you say must be the word of God. Until light permeates your heart from His word, you won't be able to produce the right sound.

A preacher who wants the supernatural to manifest must first proclaim it with his mouth. This is why, during healing meetings, preachers often make great proclamations about what the power of the Great Jehovah can do. You hear them declare confidently that blind eyes will be opened, lame will walk, the deaf will hear, etc. They are giving sound to what is in their hearts. As such proclamations are being made, supernatural forces are called into action.

Even God, the Father of the miraculous, operated this way. We are told in Genesis chapter one that a time came when God wanted a change of situation. He wanted to re-create the heavens and the earth. Darkness was everywhere; no sign of light and life. God's Spirit was hovering over the shapeless, formless and void, but that alone did not bring the desired result.

So how did God go about the task? He followed the same pattern Jesus talked about in John 3:8. *And God said...,* God produced a sound. This turned on the supernatural. As soon as God said, "Let there be light," light came. The same thing happened for every other thing He created. If God needed to produce sound to manifest His divine nature, you and I have no choice if we must manifest that same nature.

There was darkness upon the face of the deep, but God called light out of it. This means for every problem, there is a solution, but it takes a calling out for the solution to manifest. If you cannot produce the sound, don't expect the sign.

For several years, I have been making a clear sound about my health based on the revealed truth of God's Word. To the glory of God, I live in perfect health today despite my busy schedule. It is the same for every other area of life; ministry, family, etc. Like God, everything I desire (in line with God's word), I sound them out. I want protection, so I sound protection. I want a great future, so I make the same sound, and so on.

You can replace "And God said..." in Genesis 1 with "And God sounded..." I take after Him, Halleluyah! Do the same thing too. Keep saying what you desire until it comes alive and manifests physically. The supernatural response to a sound drawn out of a fountain of revealed truth. God could not have what He wanted without producing a sound, and neither can you.

Good Sound Production

Always produce a sound in your favour, using the name of Jesus. There is great power in that name. At the mention of the name, every knee bows, and every tongue confesses that He is Lord. His name is above all names. Too many Christians are producing dangerous sounds to their own hurt. Some are finding it hard to pay their house rent because all you hear them say is,

"I don't have money" or "Times are hard." They make sounds of failure, and they reap failure.

There is a great need for you to repent of the dangerous sounds you have released into the atmosphere in times past. Remember, the angels of God are at your service. They are ever-ready and are specially commissioned to execute whatever sound you produce. Angels are there to serve you; they hearken to the sound of your voice. That is why Revelation 19:10 says the angel said to John, *I am thy fellow servant and of thy brethren.* John did not know this truth and had bowed down to worship the angel earlier on!

Be careful what you say with your mouth because the angels will make sure they execute them. No wonder God's word admonishes us in Ecclesiastes 5:6:

> ***Suffer not thy mouth to cause thy flesh to sin; neither say thou before the angel, that it was an error: wherefore should God be angry at thy voice, and destroy the work of thine hands?***

Isn't that revealing? Anytime you produce sound, the miraculous takes place either in your favour or against you, depending on the kind of sound you produce.

God has given you the gift of a mouth to rule and reign in the midst of your enemies. Your mouth is a destiny-moulder.

> ***For I will give you a mouth and wisdom, which all***

your adversaries shall not be able to gainsay nor resist.

Luke 21:15

Furthermore, in Proverbs 18:21, the Bible says: *Death and Life are in the power of the tongue.* Whatever happens in your life, positive or negative is determined by the sound you produce. Every obstacle on your way is awaiting your sound (your command). The most hopeless situation will take shape at the instance of a sound drawn out of the depth of God's Word.

You Have Two Mouths!

You have two mouths: an outer and an inner mouth. The physical mouth, which can be seen, is the outer mouth, while the invisible mouth of your heart is the inner one. Several times in the earthly ministry of Jesus, He addressed the thoughts in the hearts of men. He recognised the real mouth as the one on the inside. What you say in your heart is what you actually mean, not what you say with the physical one.

What you say in your heart is more important to God than what you say with your outer mouth. The woman with the issue of blood "Said within herself" (Matthew 9:21). No wonder she got her healing. Therefore, before a miracle can take place in your life, what you say with your physical mouth must agree with what your inner mouth is saying. To say what is contrary to what your heart is saying amounts to hypocrisy.

Hannah poured out her heart to God, and only her lips moved; her words were not audible. Her heart spoke, and heaven got committed (1 Samuel 1:13). Mind what you say in your heart. That is why the Bible says, *Keep thy heart with all diligence; for out of it are the issues of life* (Proverbs 4:23).

What you think is what your inner mouth is saying, and what you speak is what your outer mouth is saying; God is committed to both. That is what Ephesians 3:20 means *Now unto him that is able to do exceeding abundantly above all that we ASK or THINK...* Your audible and inaudible voice weighs equally before God.

Some years ago, I was down physically and very weak. I was so exhausted that I could hardly lift my hand to wave down a taxi. So I said within me (in my heart), "If I can only get to the fellowship venue, no devil will be bold enough to follow me there." And you know something? That was exactly what happened. Heaven got committed to my "silent" words.

When you speak from within and speak right, God honours your word. Many Christians go about making fake confessions and end up frustrated. They say, "I have confessed it, but it has not worked." They pay more attention to their outer mouth than their inner mouth. They say "I am healed" with the outer mouth and say "This pain is killing me" with their inner mouth. So they get no result. The inner mouth is the real mouth. Concerning the

Jews, they are a very religious set of people (Always going to the temple to pray, paying tithes and offerings etc.), yet, they went into captivity. Why? *This people draweth nigh unto me with their mouth, and honoureth me with their lips; but their heart is far from me* (Matthew 15:8).

God knows that the outer mouth can be deceitful, so He pays more attention to the inner mouth. Train your inner and outer mouth to say the same thing. Note that when it comes to exercising authority over the enemy, your outer mouth must come into play. The devil does not hear what you say in your heart; he only hears and obeys what you proclaim with your physical mouth.

Luke 21:15 also implies that if a sound is produced against you, you can use your tongue to avert it. Don't forget that you must not speak just anything; speak the truth – the Word of God. The truth of God's Word spoken by a believer out of a heart of revelation moves Him to action.

So, you must be loaded with His Word and have light before making meaningful sound. If not, your sound will be void of power. You were not created for failure, defeat, sickness, oppression, etc. What makes you triumph over them is the knowledge of the truth.

When we were to have our second son some years back, the doctor said my wife would be operated on because the baby was not coming out the proper way. So I asked to see my wife. When I saw her, I said, "Child, I command you now, turn to the right position!" That was all I said, and I went home to sleep. The following day, I was told that labour ceased, and the child assumed the normal position. I came in that morning and found my wife and baby waiting for me after a normal delivery.

This is not positive thinking or psychology; it is spiritual sound dynamics. As you know, we all have a common pre-destination in Christ. He is no respecter of persons. Life is not an issue of chance; it is an issue of choice.

Choose to mature in the things of God. Load yourself with the knowledge of God's will concerning your life and produce the same sound in the face of every contrary situation. Don't be ashamed of God's Word. Say what He said about you in His Word even to the hearing of those who don't believe you. By so doing, He will definitely rise up to defend His Word.

Do you know that Goliath's head was already chopped off in the spirit realm before the physical manifestation of it? David had killed him with his words before the actual killing took place. He was too sure of God's ability to deliver, so he sounded that loud and clear. God has nothing to confirm until you give voice to the words in your heart.

> ***...I am the LORD that maketh all things... That confirmeth the word of his servant, and performeth the counsel of his messengers.***
>
> *Isaiah 44:24-26*

Make Bold Declarations

Therefore, how should you speak in line with the explanation above? In a whisper? With half your mouth closed? No! Jesus said, "What I tell you in secret, shout it on the rooftop." Boldness is the keyword here. It depicts deep-seated conviction and authority.

Do you know the secret of the great successes recorded by the apostles of old? Boldness! Acts 14:3 says:

> ***Long time therefore abode they speaking boldly in the Lord, which gave testimony unto the word of His grace, and granted signs and wonders to be done by their hands.***

They did not just speak in the Lord; they spoke boldly. This was what compelled signs and wonders to be done through their hands. The Lord confirmed His Word in their lives because of their bold speaking. For your enemies to be subdued under you, you must speak God's Word boldly. Whatever you cannot speak confidently about, don't expect to see it come to pass. Speak boldly in line with the Word of God, and you will see results. Whatever your heart desires, as long as it is covered in the Word of God, sound it out loud and boldly.

The Results of Sound

The sound you produce in line with God's Word has two major effects:

First, it forces the opposition to bow. When you keep saying what you believe, despite the happenings, the negative situation gets tired of hearing you speak against it, and so it leaves. When I was sounding prosperity, poverty was my neighbour! But after a while, it became uncomfortable with my incessant bold speaking and packed away. Now, I don't know its address. The Bible confirms this:

> ***As soon as they hear of me, they shall obey me: the strangers shall submit themselves unto me.***
>
> ***The strangers shall fade away, and be afraid out of their close places.***
>
> *Psalm 18:44-45*

Every situation and occurrence in your life that is contrary to God's Word is a stranger. As you keep producing the sound of God's will for your life, they will bow and disappear.

Secondly, the sound you produce gets heaven committed to perform. Isaiah 44:26 tells us that God confirms the words that we speak and performs our desires. Whenever you speak boldly in the Lord, you are challenging God to rise up to the occasion and defend His Word, which He has exalted above all His names (Psalm 138:2).

Think about the valley of dry bones in Ezekiel 37. Is it possible for any situation to be more hopeless than that? As Ezekiel spoke as commanded, the Prophetic sound revived that seemingly hopeless situation. That means he spoke in accordance with the Word of God. Jesus also said in Mark 11:23 that all you require to move a mountain is to produce a sound. *Say unto this mountain…* He didn't say push or cry or struggle with the mountain; He said make a prophetic sound. The mountain will definitely move as long as you do not doubt in your heart.

Friend, lose yourself from the shackles of religion. Shake off your feet from the dust and put on your beautiful divine garment. This is the truth of God's Word; embrace it and live.

Chapter Nine

The Love Command

The love factor is a very potent force in the school of signs and wonders. Wherever you find men and women, who are truly in charge of the affairs of life, you discover they are genuine lovers of God and man. Love determines your level of manifestation. If you succeed in walking in love, you have endeared yourself to God; you have won His heart, and those who win His heart make a mark on the earth. Let us examine a few of such men:

Moses

By faith Moses, when he was come to years, refused to be called the son of Pharaoh's daughter;

Choosing rather to suffer affliction with the people of God, than to enjoy the pleasures of sin for a season;

Hebrews 11:24-25

The man Moses was living in fortune; he was at peace in the palace, but his heart would not let him continue. When he saw an Egyptian maltreating one of his people, he killed him because he could not stand the people of God being humiliated. It was this love connection that gave Moses a place in the realm of the miraculous.

Elijah

> ***And he said, I have been very jealous for the Lord God of hosts: for the children of Israel have forsaken thy covenant, thrown down thine altars, and slain thy prophets with the sword; and I, even I only, am left; and they seek my life, to take it away.***
>
> *1 Kings 19:10*

When a man is in love, he is jealous over his beloved. That is why you find husbands jealous over their wives and vice versa. Elijah was jealous over the affairs of the Kingdom of God, and it earned him the right to enter the realm of miracles, signs and wonders.

He said to Ahab, *As the Lord God of Israel liveth, before whom I stand, there shall not be dew nor rain these years, but according to my word.* And it was so!

Gideon

Concerning Gideon, the Bible says the angel of God described as a mighty man of valour in Judges 6. Gideon did not celebrate his might; he celebrated his heart for

God. As a result, God caused many mighty things to happen through his hands.

Nehemiah

Nehemiah was the king's cupbearer in the land of captivity, but when he was told that the walls of Jerusalem were broken down and the people were scattered, he mourned for many days. Although he was in the palace and right at the centre of comfort and pleasure, his heart was panting after God, so God made him a captain over His people. God will make you a celebrity this end-time.

The Three Hebrew Boys

Shadrach, Meshach and Abednego preferred to die rather than bow to Nebuchadnezzar's idol. They were in love with God; their hearts were connected to Him. They went all out for Him, and God manifested Himself to them in the fire.

> ***He that hath my commandments, and keepeth them, he it is that loveth me: and he that loveth me shall be loved of my Father, and I will love him, and will manifest myself to him.***
>
> *John 14:21*

Daniel

Daniel's love for God compelled him to pray as

"aforetime," not minding the lions' den (Daniel 6). His genuine love for God caused him to be lifted supernaturally and made one of the presidents in Babylon.

Friend, you cannot be in love with God and not be promoted. You can't love Him and not make waves on the earth. It is your love connection that ultimately determines your manifestation. Daniel could not be stranded because he loved God. Therefore, you cannot love God and be stranded; He will always come to your rescue.

Love For Men

> ***If a man say, I love God, and hateth his brother, he is a liar: for he that loveth not his brother whom he hath seen, how can he love God whom he hath not seen?***
>
> *1 John 4:20*

When you claim to love God, it must reflect in your love for men; otherwise, your claim of love is fake. No one can claim to love God when he does not love his neighbour. Your love for men is a pointer to the depth of your love for God.

That is why you must guard your heart against hatred, jealousy, envy, bitterness, etc., because every evil you harbour against someone gets you stranded. Unforgiveness, bitterness, hatred, etc., disconnect you from the flow of eternal life.

Until you learn to forgive, you will remain bound and in chains. Let anyone who has offended you go; else, your prison doors will only get stronger.

> ***Whosoever hateth his brother is a murderer: and ye know that no murderer hath eternal life abiding in him.***
>
> *1 John 3:15*

In the early days of our ministry, I was to travel out of the country, but my health was in poor shape. For whatever reason, one of my associates said to somebody, "Let him go. If he dies, we will bury him." The worst thing is that he did not advise me not to go. So when I heard that, I called and asked him why he said such a thing. All I did to him was transfer him somewhere else. Today, anytime he is in town, he sleeps under my roof. That is walking in love.

Nobody can do signs without a love for God and his brethren.

> ***My little children, let us not love in word, neither in tongue; but in deed and in truth.***
>
> *1 John 3:18*

The Virtues of Love

The first virtue of walking in love is the release of ***unction***. When you are in love with God and men, you enjoy a higher degree of anointing, which is a vital force in the production of signs. The more you walk in love, the more unction you have; with greater unction, your manifestations are bound to be more.

David, a man after God's heart, loved God so much that God said concerning him:

> ***I have found David my servant; with my holy oil have I anointed him:***
>
> ***With whom my hand shall be established: mine arm also shall strengthen him.***
>
> ***The enemy shall not exact upon him; nor the son of wickedness afflict him.***
>
> ***And I will beat down his foes before his face, and plague them that hate him.***
>
> *Psalm 89:20-23*

God located a man who was truly in love with Him and anointed him. I have also discovered that the greatly anointed men of our time are men with a love connection, men of genuine love. You cannot be more anointed than you are in love with God.

As mentioned earlier, the anointing is in measures. One thing that takes you from one measure to another is love. John 3:34 tells us that Jesus was anointed without measure. But don't forget that His love for God was beyond measure as well. Until you have found a place for the love of God in your heart, you cannot command the supernatural.

In those days the multitude being very great, and having nothing to eat, Jesus called his disciples unto him, and saith unto them,

I have compassion on the multitude, because they have now been with me three days, and have nothing to eat:

And they had a few small fishes: and he blessed, and commanded to set them also before them.

So they did eat, and were filled: and they took up of the broken meat that was left seven baskets.

Mark 8:1-2,7-8

The feeding of four thousand men was a direct result of the compassion of Jesus for the multitude. He could not send them away hungry. He was filled with compassion for them, which provoked the release of the anointing and resulted in 4000 men being supernaturally fed. It was like a chain reaction — compassion provoking unction, unction guaranteeing manifestation.

It was also compassion that brought Lazarus out of the grave. When Jesus arrived at his graveside, love welled up in His heart and compelled the release of the anointing. The moment the anointing came, the desired manifestation followed.

Some years ago, a growing ministry needed to erect a church building, and I was privileged to be involved in drawing and designing it. Later, the pastor asked how much I wanted to be paid for my efforts; tears streamed down my cheeks, and I had been dreaming of when I could build houses for my God someday, not how much I should be paid for a drawing. All I kept thinking was, "Lord, if You give me money, I will build the church for them." That was all I had in my heart.

You can't love Jesus with your means and not enjoy financial miracles. It was my love for His Kingdom that motivated me into that investment, and today, I enjoy financial miracles.

You also need unction to command wealth. Deuteronomy 8:18 says:

> ***But thou shalt remember the Lord thy God: for it is he that giveth thee power to get wealth, that he may establish his covenant which he sware unto thy fathers, as it is this day.***

There is a power element involved. It is not just the work you are doing that brings the blessings, but the enabling of the Holy Spirit, which attracts favours to you.

David was an addicted lover of God; no wonder he became so blessed that he gave gold worth 576 million dollars for building the House of God. He refused to give sleep to his eyes or slumber to his eyelids until he had found a place for the God of Jacob (Psalm 132:4-5). As a result, God released the power for wealth upon him. Affection truly brings about the release of unction.

The second virtue of love is ***insight***. This is true

because it is the one you love you share your greatest secrets with. For instance, your next-door neighbour may not have access to your itinerary, but your friend who lives in another town will have a breakdown of all your activities. Likewise, God's secrets are reserved for His lovers.

> ***He made known his ways unto Moses, his acts unto the children of Israel.***
>
> *Psalm 103:7*

Jesus also said:

> ***As the Father hath loved me, so have I loved you: continue ye in my love.***
>
> ***If ye keep my commandments, ye shall abide in my love; even as I have kept my Father's commandments, and abide in his love.***
>
> ***Henceforth I call you not servants; for the servant knoweth not what his lord doeth: but I have called you friends; for all things that I have heard of my Father I have made known unto you.***
>
> *John 15:9-10,15*

It means that when you continue in His love, you are no longer treated as a servant but as a friend, and friends have access to secrets.

The more your love for God, the greater your access to depths of insight in His Word, and your depth in the Word ultimately determine your heights in life. David

Yonggi Cho once said, "Put me in a desert, and in three months, I will build a church of 10,000 members." That is not pride; but insight. He has access to secrets of church growth many do not have, so he can afford to talk like that. His depth of insight is responsible for the heights he has attained in life.

2 Timothy 2:15 says:

> ***Study to show thyself approved unto God, a workman that needeth not to be ashamed, rightly dividing the word of truth.***

It also means, "Study; get insights, and you will be approved by God as a workman, who will not be ashamed, and anything you do will prosper." The mark of approval from God was evident in Jesus' life:

> ***Ye men of Israel, hear these words; Jesus of Nazareth, a man approved of God among you by miracles and wonders and signs, which God did by him in the midst of you, as ye yourselves also know:***
>
> *Acts 2:22*

Signs and wonders are bound to follow a man of insight. The man that will command the supernatural must be a man of love. Therefore, walk in love, and you will become the miracle man you desire to be!

Chapter Ten

The Growth Command

Till we all come in the unity of the faith, and of the knowledge of the Son of God, unto a perfect man, unto the measure of the stature of the fulness of Christ:

That we henceforth be no more children, tossed to and fro, and carried about with every wind of doctrine, by the sleight of men, and cunning craftiness, whereby they lie in wait to deceive;

But speaking the truth in love, may grow up into him in all things, which is the head, even Christ:

Ephesians 4:13-15

Growth in the Kingdom of God is not optional but mandatory. If you don't grow, you will groan. However, while some people are growing, others are busy looking for shortcuts – they want to jump up. But I have observed that if you jump up, you will come down, but if you grow up, you will stay up! Someone wisely said that there is no shortcut to any place worth going.

Growth is a must if the miraculous is your desire. It is the extent to which you develop that determines whether God can entrust you with signs and wonders or not.

When Jesus, the Messiah, came to the earth, He carried the fullness of the Godhead bodily, yet, He was a child and could not manifest His glory.

> ***And* the child grew, *and waxed strong in spirit, filled with wisdom: and the grace of God was upon him.***
>
> Luke 2:40

Jesus began as a child, but He did not stop there; He developed physically (*and the child grew)*, spiritually (*and waxed strong in the spirit*), and mentally (*filled with wisdom*). Jesus grew in the three dimensions of human existence.

When Jesus grew into a Son, it was written concerning Him that He returned in the power of the Spirit (Luke 4:14). It was after then He could take His rightful place and exercise authority as the Son of God.

We all begin our Christian adventure as children of God, but not all remain children. Some become sons of God, others graduate into men of God, and others grow to become messengers of God until they ultimately become friends of God. All these are reflections of the various levels of growth.

Yes, you are an heir of God and a joint heir with Christ, but you cannot handle certain things at the level you are now until you grow up more than where you are now.

As important as growth is to the Body of Christ, so little attention has been paid to it in the charismatic circles that many are groaning under the things they are not grown enough to handle.

Do you give your eight-year-old child your car keys to drive your car? By heritage, the car may be his, but as long as he is underage, he is not permitted to drive. But when that same child becomes eighteen, he becomes a co-owner of your car and can drive it anytime he wants. Similarly, when you mature as a Christian, many of the things you are crying for now will simply be at your disposal.

Apostle Paul tells us that there are weights of glory.

> ***For our light affliction, which is but for a moment, worketh for us a far more exceeding and eternal weight of glory;***
>
> *2 Corinthians 4:17*

> ***There is one glory of the sun, and another glory of the moon, and another glory of the stars: for one star differeth from another star in glory.***
>
> *1 Corinthians 15:41*

No matter the weight of glory you desire, it is available in God, but you must grow to match. From a son, Jesus grew to a point He was equal with God. He could actually say, *I and my Father are one.* But that was not where He started. Please understand that growth is a continuous process; when you stop growing you start dying.

Growing in Grace

> ***But by the grace of God I am what I am: and his grace which was bestowed upon me was not in vain; but I laboured more abundantly than they all: yet not I, but the grace of God which was with me.***
>
> *1 Corinthians 15:10*

Grace is indispensable in the making of any man; it determines how high you rise in this Kingdom. That is why Paul said, "But by the grace of God I am what I am." What you want to become will require grace.

However, this grace can be multiplied through the knowledge of God. Apostle Paul, a man made by grace, worked on his level of grace as he desperately searched the Word of God. He was a hungry seeker of knowledge. As he grew in his knowledge of God, he also increased in grace.

> ***But* grow in grace, *and in the knowledge of our Lord and Saviour Jesus Christ...***
>
> *2 Peter 3:18*

Grace and peace be multiplied unto you through the knowledge of God, and of Jesus our Lord,

2 Peter 1:2

Your status is a function of growth. If you want greater grace, you must aim at greater growth.

Growing in Faith

For I say, through the grace given unto me, to every man that is among you, not to think of himself more highly than he ought to think; but to think soberly, according as God hath dealt to every man the measure of faith.

Romans 12:3

Faith is in measures; what you do with the measure of faith you have now will determine whether you move up to the next level or not. The first measure of faith is given to a man at new birth (in fact, it is impossible to be saved without faith).

For by grace are ye saved through faith; and that not of yourselves: it is the gift of God:

Ephesians 2:8

At salvation, you receive a measure of faith. However, this measure can be lost; as such, you return to a **no-faith** realm.

And he said unto them, Why are ye so fearful? how is it that ye have no faith?

Mark 4:40

The ten virgins had a measure of oil at the beginning, but out of carelessness, five of them allowed their measure to run out. So when the bridegroom came in the middle of the night, they did not have any oil to meet him. That means no matter how strong your faith is now, unless you guard it jealously, you can lose it.

The next level is the **little faith** level. In this group are those who have done little with their measure of faith.

> ***Wherefore, if God so clothe the grass of the field, which to day is, and tomorrow is cast into the oven, shall he not much more clothe you, O ye of little faith?***
>
> *Matthew 6:30*

There is also another level of faith called **great faith.** In this group are those who have done great things with their faith.

> ***When Jesus heard it, he marvelled, and said to them that followed, Verily I say unto you, I have not found so great faith, no, not in Israel.***
>
> *Matthew 8:10*

From that point, you enter into exceeding growing faith.

> ***We are bound to thank God always for you, brethren, as it is meet, because that your faith groweth exceedingly, and the charity of every one***

of you all toward each other aboundeth;
2 Thessalonians 1:3

The next level of faith is grounded and settled faith. At this point, you are like Mount Zion that cannot be moved but abideth forever; you enter into the realm of trust.

If ye continue in the faith grounded and settled, and be not moved away from the hope of the gospel, which ye have heard, and which was preached to every creature which is under heaven...
Colossians 1:23

All these are proofs that faith is a living force because only living things grow. But it is also true that whatever grows dies. Therefore, the faith that grows can also die, except you learn how to nurture it. How do you nurture your faith? By the Word of God (Romans 10:17).

Growing in The Word

So mightily grew the word of God and prevailed.
Acts 19:20

Mighty growth in the Word will result into mighty acts (Acts 19:11-12). So, Word-growth equals sign-growth. As you consistently feed on the Word of God – not haphazardly, not as convenient, it will result in mighty growth. A disciplined and consistent approach to the study of the Word of God is the cheapest way up. You will go up!

Friend, it is time to pay "mighty" attention to the Word because mighty attention will lead to mighty manifestations. Just get ready because when the Word of God in you increases, there is bound to be an explosion of signs and wonders. Therefore, if you want to see mighty acts, go for a mighty Word growth.

Growing in The Anointing

You can also grow in the anointing of the Holy Ghost (Ezekiel 47:1-5). For example, Jesus had an encounter with the Holy Ghost in Matthew 3:16, when the Holy Ghost came upon Him as a dove. Later in chapter four, He went to the wilderness and came back in the power of the Spirit. At another time, He went up into a high mountain and was transfigured. His raiment became glistering white, and his face dazzled. Jesus grew in the anointing until the devil could not stand His presence.

The apostles also grew in the anointing. In Acts 2, they were baptised in the Holy Ghost, and later in Chapter 4, they were again anointed with the Spirit. All of these reflect various degrees of the infilling of the Holy Spirit.

David Yonggi Cho wrote in one of his books, "Growth means change." Growth calls for a change in approach and attitude. Until you make room for positive changes in your life, you cannot be said to be growing. It is the tangible changes that reflect how much you are growing.

For instance, physically, you must have changed a great deal from your primary school days. Whatever pictures you took back then will not look like you anymore. That is change; that is growth.

Leave The Fundamentals

> ***Therefore leaving the principles of the doctrine of Christ, let us go on unto perfection; not laying again the foundation of repentance from dead works, and of faith toward God,***
>
> ***Of the doctrine of baptisms, and of laying on of hands, and of resurrection of the dead, and of eternal judgment.***
>
> *Hebrews 6:1-2*

There are fundamental issues also known as elementary principles of the doctrine of Christ, which you must leave to move on to a higher realm in God. It is a realm where you taste of the powers of the world to come. You appear to be living beyond your generation, far beyond the level your colleagues are. It is the unlimited realm, where nothing says "no" to you; as you step in, everything contrary steps out.

Apostle Paul operated in this realm of encounters, the realm he would speak, and the Holy Ghost would put His stamp of approval on it. That is a realm above doctrines; it is a realm of encounters.

God's will is that we grow from grace to grace, glory

to glory, faith to faith, anointing to anointing, but this can only be possible as we are changed from one realm of glory to another.

> ***But we all, with open face beholding as in a glass the glory of the Lord, are changed into the same image from glory to glory, even as by the Spirit of the Lord.***
>
> *2 Corinthians 3:18*

Friend, your inheritance in God can only be delivered to you at the degree of your growth in Him. So, make up your mind to stop waiting and start growing.

Chapter Eleven

The Name Command

To the rest of the world, there may not be anything in a name, but not to Biblical Christianity. Right from the Old Testament to the New Testament, it is discovered that there is everything in a name. For instance, Concerning Nabal, the husband of Abigail, he was reputed for foolish behaviour:

> ***Let not my lord, I pray thee, regard this man of Belial, even Nabal: for as his name is, so is he; Nabal is his name, and folly is with him: but I thine handmaid saw not the young men of my lord, whom thou didst send.***
>
> *1 Samuel 25:25*

He lived up to his name and died a foolish man. In Bible history, names symbolised the commission of their bearer. Everyone manifested his name. Thus, many Bible characters had their names changed to suit their commission or covenant with God. God changed Sarai to Sarah, which meant Princess, to match her new status. Jacob, the trickster, was changed to Israel, which means Prince.

When Jesus was here, He changed the name of His disciples to suit their assignments. James and John, the sons of Zebedee, were surnamed Boarnerges, which means the sons of thunder. Simon (Peter) was renamed Cephas, the stone.

> ***And he brought him to Jesus. And when Jesus beheld him, he said, Thou art Simon the son of Jona: thou shalt be called Cephas, which is by interpretation, A stone.***
>
> *John 1:42*

Until then, Peter was identified as an unstable character. However, because of the commission given to him, he needed the toughness or ruggedness of a stone to stand in his office. Apostle Paul was formerly known as Saul of Tarsus. Nevertheless, at his conversion, everything became new, including his name. He needed a new identity to carry out his assignment.

However, it is in the life of Jesus Himself that we are to see in clear relief the use of names as significant indicators of a commission. Take a look at this prophecy heralding His birth:

> ***For unto us a child is born, unto us a son is given: and the government shall be upon his shoulder: and***

his name shall be called Wonderful, Counsellor, The mighty God, The everlasting Father, The Prince of Peace.

Isaiah 9:6

Many think the name of Jesus is a mere pause in prayer or just a symbol of identification. Much as the name performs these functions, the name, most importantly, provides a trigger for the manifestation of all that characterises that name.

Isaiah's prophecy delineates certain qualities, which the name should manifest at invocation. First, the name is full of wonders. This means when His name is invoked in faith, wonderful things happen. During His earthly ministry, by His name, evil men and demons were threatened. At His presence, demons cried out His name and left their victims. Before His ascension, He gave the authority to His disciples to use His name to command the supernatural:

And these signs shall follow them that believe; In my name shall they cast out devils; they shall speak with new tongues;

They shall take up serpents; and if they drink any deadly thing, it shall not hurt them; they shall lay hands on the sick, and they shall recover.

Mark 16:17-18

All the signs mentioned above are supernatural in nature. So Jesus means to say that when His name is invoked, you will do things beyond the natural realm. His name will cause any sign to become manifest. The same meaning is portrayed in John 14:13: *Whatsoever ye ask in my name, that will I do...* So whatever thing you desire, no matter how impossible it seems, will surely come to pass when the name of Jesus is used in faith. Therefore, this is a call to give up the "impossibility syndrome." Nothing is impossible to those who know the power in that name. So whatever anybody has said about your situation will become irrelevant, and you won't need to cry the way you do.

Consider this example from Acts chapter three, when Peter and John were on their way to the temple. They were faced with a humanly impossible situation; they met a lame man who needed their help. Evidently, they were cash-strapped but realised they had something more than cash – the name of Jesus.

> ***Then Peter said, Silver and gold have I none; but such as I have give I thee: In the name of Jesus Christ of Nazareth rise up and walk.***
>
> *Acts 3:6*

Peter simply pressed the trigger, the supernatural was released, and the man walked. Halleluyah! You don't beg with the name; you reign with it. You can destroy every disease, sickness or anything that detracts from the redemptive package with that name when mentioned in faith.

Faith in the name is what propels its efficacy. When the seven sons of Sceva, exorcists, tried to toy with the name, they were cast out(Acts 19:14-16). Faith in the name guarantees its efficacy! If you want to become a commander of wonders, learn to use the name in faith.

Still on the Isaiah prophecy, counsel is released at the mention of the name of Jesus, thereby showing you the right path to follow. Counsel is an integral element of wisdom, and you need wisdom to manifest as a son of God. Every enterprise is established by counsel.

The name equally releases might – He is the mighty God. So when the name is invoked, the might of God is manifested. Strength comes in the place of weakness and excitement, and confidence comes in the place of frustration and despondency.

Similarly, the name of Jesus manifests the eternal nature of God. It is the release of the life of God that makes living in the supernatural possible for the believer. God's nature is in the supernatural. At the invocation of the name, there is a manifestation that makes the supernatural a cheap possibility.

Invocation of the name of Jesus also compels peace, which is a requirement for flowing in the realm of the supernatural. He is the Prince of Peace, and He is committed to fighting for only those who know how to hold their peace. The invocation of His name in faith will establish peace in your heart for the manifestation of the supernatural.

Genesis of The Name

The name of Jesus is an all-purpose name. It provides a covering for all things in the life of a believer. Not a few must be intrigued at the potency of the name and perhaps would wonder how this came to be. In this section, we will examine how Jesus came about the greatness or almightiness attached to His name.

By Prophecy

Before Jesus was born, several prophecies went forth concerning the birth of the messiah. When angel Gabriel appeared to Joseph to intimate him about the conception of Jesus by his wife Mary, he declared:

> ***And she shall bring forth a son, and thou shalt call his name JESUS: for he shall save his people from their sins.***
>
> *Matthew 1:21*

The cardinal mission of Jesus is to save all men from sin. As mentioned earlier, sin ruptured the link between man and God. So sin is at the root of man's problems, and until the sin problem is dealt with, the solution to any human problem is not in view.

> ***Neither is there salvation in any other: for there is none other name under heaven given among men, whereby we must be saved.***
>
> *Acts 4:12*

The name of Jesus is the only authentic solution to the problem of sin. You can't handle that habit you so much want to give up by your power. New year resolutions and willpower are unhelpful. Until you use the name, your deliverance is not guaranteed. Apart from the angel's announcement of the mission of Jesus, other prophets of God had also foretold it in diverse prophecies. Isaiah was the foremost of them. In Isaiah 11:1-2, we have this very profound prophecy about the Messiah.

> ***And there shall come forth a*** *rod* ***out of the stem of Jesse, and a Branch shall grow out of his roots:***
>
> ***And the spirit of the LORD shall rest upon him, the spirit of wisdom and understanding...***

The object of this prophecy cannot be mistaken. It shows us the picture of Jesus. The rod is a direct reference to Him. Now cast your mind back to Moses in the book of Exodus. He was the man with the rod. God told him:

> ***And thou shalt take this rod in thine hand, wherewith thou shalt do signs.***
>
> *Exodus 4:17*

The rod of Moses was the rod of authority. Without the rod, Moses was incapacitated; he was as powerless as every other man in Egypt and could not move an ant. However, with the rod, he was a terror to Pharaoh and the whole land of Egypt. The rod of Moses was a multi-purpose rod. It swallowed the magician's rods that turned into serpents. When he stretched it towards the rivers of Egypt, the waters turned to blood. When he pointed it to the sky, thunder, hail, and fire was the outcome. It was with the rod he parted the Red Sea for the children of Israel to cross over.

Everything Moses wanted came to be with the rod. The rod distinguished Moses; it conferred on him honour and awe in all of Egypt. Comparing spiritual things with spiritual, just like Moses used a physical rod to establish his dominion in Egypt, believers have a spiritual rod, which is the name of Jesus, to establish their dominion on earth. As Moses was commanded to do signs with his rod, signs are to follow the believers in the name of Jesus.

If the rod distinguished Moses, the name of Jesus would distinguish you. The name is the greatest asset in the life of any believer. You have the license to use it to dislodge any evil hanging around your life, family or business.

By Conquest

Jesus also got His Omnipotent name by conquest. Through His death and resurrection, He completely triumphed over the devil and his host of demons. He made a mess of them and disposed them of their power.

Forasmuch then as the children are partakers of flesh and blood, he also himself likewise took part of the same; that through death he might destroy him that had the power of death, that is, the devil;

And deliver them who through fear of death were all their lifetime subject to bondage.

Hebrews 2:14-15

His conquest established our redemption from the oppressive dominion of the devil. Through His name, believers have been given the authority to deal with any intimidation and harassment of the devil. Whatever threatens the enjoyment of your redemptive privileges can be overcome through the name. It is the master key to all of life's circumstances. Don't just call the name; use it!

By Inheritance

Jesus was the first begotten of the Father. He got His omnipotent name by inheritance. Not even the angels in their entire splendor could inherit that name. God gave it to Him as a mark of honour for His distinguished position in the Godhead as the Redeemer of mankind.

Being made so much better than the angels, as he hath by inheritance obtained a more excellent name than they.

For unto which of the angels said he at any time, Thou art my Son, this day have I begotten thee?

> ***And again, I will be to him a Father, and he shall be to me a Son?***
>
> *Hebrews 1:4-5*

By His redemptive grace, every believer is made a "joint heir" with Christ. He gave us the name of Jesus as a staff of office. If you are a believer, what He has, you have. He has given you His name for your possession. It is a name to possess, not just to know. Whatever you demand from God by covenant with Jesus, He has no choice but to grant it. His name gives you access to a mysterious lifestyle that should reflect His glory and majesty here on earth.

By Obedience

Obedience was the key element that earned Jesus His omnipotent name. He was obedient to the will of the Father, even unto death. He suffered shame and humiliation at the hands of sinners, but nothing could distract Him from the goal of redemption. With unparalleled obedience, He accomplished His assignment.

> ***Wherefore God also hath highly exalted him, and given him a name which is above every name:***
>
> ***That at the name of Jesus every knee should bow, of things in heaven, and things in earth, and things under the earth;***
>
> ***And that every tongue should confess that Jesus***

Christ is Lord, to the glory of God the Father.
Philippians 2:9-11

Obedience earned for Jesus, the most exalted name in heaven, on earth or under the earth. Everything and every name answers to it. Think of this: Death is a name. Barrenness is a name. Failure is a name. Unemployment and poverty are also names. Whatever has a name is compelled to bow when the name of Jesus is invoked.

What that means is that at the invocation of the name, all the heavenly forces ensure that the purpose for which the name was invoked is accomplished. At the name, every force of opposition in all the realms of existence surrenders. You can use the name to level all your mountains (oppositions). You can use the name to establish your health or turn around your financial destiny. You can use the name to restore peace, love and joy to your marriage. You can use the name to manifest the very nature of God. It is a multi-purpose solution to any problem.

Because it is a gift, its potency can never depreciate because "The gifts and callings of God are without repentance." It remains steadfast as the authority to which every other thing bows. You can put a divine seal on all affairs of your life by doing all things in the name of the Lord.

Chapter Twelve

The Prayer Command

Elias was a man subject to like passions as we are, and he prayed earnestly that it might not rain: and it rained not on the earth by the space of three years and six months.

And he prayed again, and the heaven gave rain, and the earth brought forth her fruit.

James 5:17-18

There is a type of prayer that provokes the release of signs and wonders. It is neither long drawn nor accomplished by shouting; it is called the prayer that avails much. This kind of prayer releases tremendous power, which is dynamic in working. The Amplified Bible describes it as:

...The earnest (heartfelt, continued) prayer of a righteous man makes tremendous power available

[dynamic in its working].

James 5:16

It is this type of prayer that triggers the miraculous. There are times you pray, and as the prayer is leaving your lips, you know it is nothing but a religious rite because it is not arriving at God's throne. But when your whole being is involved in praying, you attract heaven's attention.

It is not how long you pray that matters but how well. Look at some Biblical examples:

Hannah

Hannah's case was pitiful: she had been married for many years but did not have a child. To make matters worse, she also had a rival who provoked her sore. Tormented and afflicted, Hannah went before God and poured out her heart to the Lord.

And she vowed a vow, and said, O Lord of hosts, if thou wilt indeed look on the affliction of thine handmaid, and remember me, and not forget thine handmaid, but wilt give unto thine handmaid a man child, then I will give him unto the Lord all the days of his life, and there shall no razor come upon his head.

And it came to pass, as she continued praying before the Lord, that Eli marked her mouth.

Now Hannah, she spake in her heart; only her lips

moved, but her voice was not heard: therefore Eli thought she had been drunken.

And Eli said unto her, How long wilt thou be drunken? put away thy wine from thee.

And Hannah answered and said, No, my lord, I am a woman of a sorrowful spirit: I have drunk neither wine nor strong drink, but have poured out my soul before the Lord.

...And Elkanah knew Hannah his wife; and the Lord remembered her.

1 Samuel 1:11-15,19

Her mouth moved as she prayed, but nobody could hear her because she was praying from her heart! Because the scriptures cannot be broken, her heart-seated effectual prayer released enough power to break the chains of barrenness. There is what to say from your heart that will change your destiny.

Friend, your case is finally settled! Those tears you have shed in secret over that case of barrenness shall be wiped away this time, in Jesus' name.

Hezekiah

In Isaiah 38, King Hezekiah was sick unto death, and God sent the prophet Isaiah to inform him he would surely die. You must understand that in his time, Isaiah was God's recognised mouthpiece; whatever he said carried heaven's stamp of approval. Yet, even after

Isaiah's visit, Hezekiah refused to give up; he turned his face to the wall and cried to God, and the answer came speedily.

> ***In those days was Hezekiah sick unto death. And Isaiah the prophet the son of Amoz came unto him, and said unto him, Thus saith the Lord, Set thine house in order: for thou shalt die, and not live.***
>
> ***Then Hezekiah turned his face toward the wall, and prayed unto the Lord,***
>
> ***And said, Remember now, O Lord, I beseech thee, how I have walked before thee in truth and with a perfect heart, and have done that which is good in thy sight. And Hezekiah wept sore.***
>
> ***Then came the word of the Lord to Isaiah, saying,***
>
> ***Go, and say to Hezekiah, Thus saith the Lord, the God of David thy father, I have heard thy prayer, I have seen thy tears: behold, I will add unto thy days fifteen years.***
>
> ***And I will deliver thee and this city out of the hand of the king of Assyria: and I will defend this city.***
>
> *Isaiah 38:1-6*

His prayer could not have been more than 60 seconds, yet, it caught heaven's attention. There is no point playing the religion of futility. Even if you have been praying for 19 days, it does not automatically result in answers. What is most vital is that your prayer connects the throne of God. Once that connection is made, signs come straight away. Hezekiah adopted the wise approach to prayer based on Isaiah 43:26:

> ***Put me in remembrance: let us plead together: declare thou, that thou mayest be justified.***

He reminded God of how he had walked with Him with a perfect heart, and that did it. God sent Isaiah back to cancel what He had earlier said.

There is no need for showmanship in prayer. It is not how well you can compose prayers for people's applause, but rather, praying a prayer that comes from the depth of your heart. I believe Hezekiah did not ask Isaiah to join him in a prayer of agreement. He knew he had access to God by himself, and as he used that access, God added fifteen more years to his life. This is how to gain access to God's hotline for a release of the miraculous.

Elijah

Elijah had a very profound ministry backed up by signs and wonders. He is also a reference point for effectual prayer. While the priests of Baal were cutting themselves with knives, crying and shouting, Elijah simply prayed for about 60 seconds or thereabout, and the fire of the Lord fell, consuming the burnt offering, water, wood and stones! His prayer was short but heart-seated, so it connected with the source, and a miracle followed.

> ***And it came to pass at the time of the offering of the evening sacrifice, that Elijah the prophet came near, and said, Lord God of Abraham, Isaac, and of Israel, let it be known this day that thou art God in Israel, and that I am thy servant, and that I have done all these things at thy word.***
>
> ***Hear me, O Lord, hear me, that this people may know that thou art the Lord God, and that thou hast turned their heart back again.***
>
> *1 Kings 18:36-37*

Jesus

The prayer Jesus made that raised Lazarus from the dead was just a few seconds long, yet, it had enough power to bring a dead man back to life.

> ***Then they took away the stone from the place where the dead was laid. And Jesus lifted up his eyes, and said,* Father, I thank thee that thou hast heard me.**
>
> *John 11:41*

Prayer is not a religious jamboree. You can settle down and set yourself to connect with the throne of God. Once you position your heart aright, you will never miss your target in prayer.

All the connections I have taught so far are vital in making your prayer gain access to God. The name of Jesus guarantees your access to God, purity ensures the sustenance of that access, and faith assures you of results.

The Word gives you confidence that God cannot turn you back, and the Holy Spirit helps your infirmity when you are disorganised and don't know what to pray about so you can hit your target correctly. It is a whole network.

Chapter Thirteen

The Praise Command

Praise is a formidable tool in the working of miracles. Though often paid the least attention, it is as potent as prayer. Looking at Jesus' ministry, the two most profound miracles He did were as a result of thanksgiving. When He was to feed 5,000 men in the wilderness, thanksgiving multiplied the loaves (John 6:5-12), and at the graveside of Lazarus, praise brought him back to life (John 11:41-44).

Praise has multiplication power; therefore, this praise connection is intended to usher you into realms of unlimited signs and wonders.

> ***And Jesus took the loaves; and when he had given thanks, he distributed to the disciples, and the disciples to them that were set down; and likewise of the fishes as much as they would.***
>
> ***When they were filled, he said unto his disciples,***

Gather up the fragments that remain, that nothing be lost.

Therefore they gathered them together, and filled twelve baskets with the fragments of the five barley loaves, which remained over and above unto them that had eaten.

John 6:11-13

Among other things, praise has an inherent miracle force that ensures nothing finishes in your hand. God need to open your eyes to the power of praise; once you grasp it, all your struggles will come to an end.

It is still difficult for me to explain how we fed in my home on an income of ₦440 a month (I was on ₦300, and my wife was on 140), yet, we never dipped our hands into church funds. Meanwhile, we always had a crowd of people living with us, yet, we never lacked food. Where the money was coming from, I could not explain except to acknowledge it must have come from heaven.

I remember when I was a bachelor, I lived in a one-room apartment, and sometimes, I had as many as eight people staying with me, yet, we never came to a point where we were looking around for what to eat. Not once!

Friend, there is a fountain you connect to in thanksgiving that ensures you never run dry. If businessmen and women will hook up to that fountain, they will encounter the multiplication power of praise.

> ***Let the people praise thee, O God; let all the people praise thee.***
>
> ***Then shall the earth yield her increase; and God, even our own God, shall bless us.***
>
> *Psalm 67:3,6*

The power in praise is released as you praise God. At every point and in whatever situation you find yourself in, still give Him thanks.

Praise Is His Will

> ***In every thing give thanks: for this is the will of God in Christ Jesus concerning you.***
>
> *1 Thessalonians 5:18*

> ***Cast not away therefore your confidence, which hath great recompense of reward.***
>
> ***For ye have need of patience, after ye have done the will of God, ye might receive the promise***
>
> *Hebrews 10:35-36*

Praise is the will of God, and after you have done His will, you are sure to obtain the promise of signs and wonders. God's promise is that signs should follow you, but this promise will not be accomplished until you first do God's will, which is praise. Therefore, no matter what you are going through, praise Him, and you will obtain the promise.

Praise is not just one of those preparatory things you do before prayer. It has a force of its own, which is able to produce signs and wonders. If it could bring Lazarus, who had been dead for four days, back to life, it can bring you into a strange order of manifestations.

In Liberia, one of our Bible School students decided to operate what she had been taught about the wonders of praise. It was during the war, and there was no food; everyone was literally starving. But as she was praising God, a group of rebels suddenly invaded their compound. They entered her house, but instead of harming them, they brought bags of rice, beans, chicken and other food items and said, "Cook for us." The rebels ate that day and left, leaving the rest of the bags of food behind. God miraculously supplied their need.

That is why God's Word says, *In everything, give thanks, for this is the will of God concerning you.*

Praise Attracts God's Presence

> ***But thou art holy, O thou that inhabitest the praises of Israel.***
>
> *Psalm 22:3*

God inhabits the praises of His people. So when you live a praiseful life, God's presence abides with you; when He abides with you, He compels signs to attend to you.

You have been alone in that shop that is why things are the way they are. Why not bring God there through your praises and see the difference? Divine presence equals signs and wonders.

In Psalm 114, when the children of Israel came out of Egypt, God was their sanctuary. The sea saw them and fled, Jordan was driven back, and the mountains skipped like rams, the little hills like young lambs. God's presence took them through the Red Sea and gave them victory over their enemies. When you succeed in invoking divine presence, you live as a sign and wonder to your generation.

In Acts 16, Paul and Silas were about to be executed; they were in the mid-night of their lives, but the Bible says they prayed and sang praises aloud to God in prison (they turned on their praise connection right in the midst of their executioners), and something happened!

Friend, those men sang God into that place! As He came, there was an earthquake; the prison gates flung open, and their chains fell off! They were so confident they could perform the same feat again that they did not bother to escape from the prison. They knew that what had happened did not come by chance. When praise becomes your lifestyle, you never cease commanding signs.

In 2 Chronicles 20, King Jehoshaphat stepped back and allowed God to go ahead. God took their place in battle, and victory was sure.

> ***Ye shall not need to fight in this battle: set yourselves, stand ye still, and see the salvation of the Lord***

with you, O Judah and Jerusalem: fear not, nor be dismayed; tomorrow go out against them: for the Lord will be with you.

2 Chronicles 20:17

How did they set themselves? In praises! Praise causes God to fight on your behalf — He takes your place in battle while you just watch. Praise compels Him to take over the battles of your life. This is a covenant technique that guarantees cheap victory. You don't have to be strong to succeed; just be smart. Praise is the choice of the smart.

There is no mountain God's presence cannot level, no sea He cannot dry up and no "Jordan" that cannot be driven back so that you can have an express way to your destination. However, praise is your access to His presence. Once you engage in praise, you have brought Him to bear on the situations of your life, and all things will be at your command.

I have seen many prayer warriors who are praise-dry. Prayer is important, but when you pray, all you have access to is angelic intervention. And angels can be waylaid by demons, as was the case with Daniel. However, praise does not stop at angels; it brings the presence of God Almighty down, and when God steps somewhere, no demon can stop Him or stand in His way.

Friend, it does not matter what situation you find yourself in right now, receive grace to praise Him.

This may shock you, but I have not had to pray for my personal needs since I came into ministry. I am always so thankful for everything He has done, so He never waits for me to ask for a thing before He blesses me. His presence is equal to the task of providing for any man's needs.

Steer Clear of Murmuring

> ***And when the people complained, it displeased the Lord: and the Lord heard it; and his anger was kindled; and the fire of the Lord burnt among them, and consumed them that were in the uttermost parts of the camp.***
>
> *Numbers 11:1*

God hates murmurers. Those who murmured in the wilderness were destroyed by the destroyer. Their murmuring and complaining turned God against them, and if God is against you, what are you worth? That is why those who murmur are natural failures; nothing works in their hands, so they live in perpetual struggles.

This is the bane of many believers today. They work so hard, but nothing is working because God's presence that makes things work is far from them.

A heart of gratitude is your fastest escape from the trap of murmuring. Gratitude will cause God's presence to envelop you, causing signs to attend to your every step. You cannot live a sign-dry life when you are full of gratitude. It is a great asset for the miraculous. Jesus said in John 8:29:

And he that sent me is with me: the Father hath not left me alone; for I do always those things that please him.

And what is the one thing that pleases God? It is found in Psalm 69:30-31.

I will praise the name of God with a song, and will magnify him with thanksgiving.

This also shall please the Lord better than an ox or bullock that hath horns and hoofs.

Praise pleases God, and when He is pleased, He releases all manner of signs and wonders to follow you.

Praise is one of the vital keys for the release of the supernatural. An understanding of its place in supernatural living will always cause you to flow in the miraculous. The supernatural will become natural.

Friend, the will of God is for you to give thanks in everything. In Hebrew 10:36, the Bible says that we obtain the promise only after we have done His will of God. Until you do His will, don't expect to obtain the promise. But as you do it, every obstacle will begin to give way. I have proved this for several years, and it works. It will work for you!

Chapter Fourteen

The Fellowship Command

But upon mount Zion shall be deliverance, and there shall be holiness; and the house of Jacob shall possess their possessions.

Obadiah 1:17

Every trade has its training centre. To train as a technician, you go to a technical school. To be trained as a driver, you go to a driving school. Until you are trained, you don't triumph. In the same vein, to be trained up for signs, you have to go to Zion. Zion is our training ground, our school for signs.

Yes, you are created for signs, but until you are trained, you cannot manifest it. God has declared that upon Mount Zion there shall be deliverance and holiness, and the house of Jacob shall possess their possessions. That means Zion is a place your inheritance is handed over to you. It is a place of deliverance from every oppression of hell, a place you are cleaned up, and whatever belongs to you is delivered to you.

Zion is a spiritual factory for signs. It is where signs are produced en masse. Remember that before the coming of Jesus, it was declared:

> ***Therefore the Lord himself shall give you a sign; Behold, a virgin shall conceive, and bear a son, and shall call his name Immanuel.***
>
> *Isaiah 7:14*

Jesus' coming was a sign. He was a sign from heaven, and as the Father has sent Him, so has He sent us. That is why we too are signs to our generation. Jesus came as a Saviour, and the Bible says we too are saviours. Therefore, by spiritual calculations, saviours are signs, and they are released from Zion. Thus, the Kingdom of God is established by the ministry of saviours.

That is why somebody anoints the dead, and he jerks back to life. That is a sign, and a pointer to the end-time ministry of the Church because the last enemy to be destroyed is death (1 Corinthians 15:26).

Friend, we have come into the days of saviours, and they are made in Zion. Therefore, the more addicted you are to Zion, the higher your status in the class of saviours. Remember that stars differ in glory.

After the Holy Ghost's arrival on the day of Pentecost, one of the things He introduced was a strong love for fellowship among the disciples. They assembled daily in the temple and met in various houses.

The result of this was the rise of great men of faith from among them. Men like Stephen, who was appointed as a deacon to serve tables. But as he stayed with them in fellowship, he began to grow in the power of the Holy Ghost and faith until he exploded in signs and wonders. Stephen came out of Zion as a saviour.

> ***And they, continuing daily with one accord in the temple, and breaking bread from house to house, did eat their meat with gladness and singleness of heart.***
>
> *Acts 2:46*

> ***And Stephen, full of faith and power, did great wonders and miracles among the people.***
>
> *Acts 6:8*

In Acts 8, we also see Philip doing exploits in the city of Samaria. He too was a product of the teachings of the apostles. Therefore, as you give the Word you are being taught in Zion its rightful place in your heart and life, someday, you too will explode in signs, wonders and miracles.

Once you locate a place where the Word is preached in truth and plug into the happenings there, you have registered in the school of signs. Someday, you will find yourself performing signs and wonders, blessing your generation in areas like business, career, ministry, etc. You will suddenly break loose, and your generation will glorify God for you.

You are for signs and wonders, and the Church is there to help make it a reality. Not just every place is called "church," but places where God's Word is taught, and you are shown how to stand in your place in the covenant. That is why Hebrews 10:25 says:

> ***Not forsaking the assembling of ourselves together, as the manner of some is; but exhorting one another: and so much the more, as ye see the day approaching.***

As Jesus' second coming draws closer, fellowship will become more and more necessary for everyone who wants to be current in the move of God. By God's prophetic agenda, we shall see our enemies completely under our feet these last days, and when God has accomplished that, then Jesus will return. Fellowship is not a place to play with this end-time. To stay away from it is to fall away from God's end-time programme.

What Is In Zion?

> ***But ye are come unto mount Sion, and unto the city of the living God, the heavenly Jerusalem, and to an innumerable company of angels,***
>
> ***To the general assembly and church of the firstborn, which are written in heaven, and to God the Judge of all, and to the spirits of just men made perfect,***
>
> ***And to Jesus the mediator of the new covenant,***

and to the blood of sprinkling, that speaketh better things than that of Abel.

Hebrews 12:22-24

Coming to church is not coming to human society. Zion is the mountain of God; it is the habitation of Jehovah. It is the city of the living God. That is why you can rush to the church at any time you are faced with a challenge, whether there is a service going on or not, and you will meet with solutions because Zion is God's city; that is where He has chosen to put His name, His throne is there also.

Until you are conscious of where you are, you can never get the best out of it. That was how a lady with a tumour sitting upon her eye nerves was miraculously healed when she rushed into Zion.

In February 1996, I realised I could not see well with my eyes. Though I have been wearing glasses, and even with them, I still could not see well. It was as if something very strong or dark was in my front whenever I looked up. So, when I went to London for my daughter's graduation, I decided to see my optician. Some tests were carried out, and the difference between my last results and the one just done was so much.

The doctor asked me to go for more X-rays, and I did. After a close examination, they took me into a large machine, which was large as a hall. At the end of the test, they found a tumour sitting right on top of one of my eye nerves. The doctor tried to explain it to me by drawing a diagram and said it was the reason I could not see well.

He further said the tumour had to be removed immediately; otherwise, my brain would be filled with blood, and I would be blind in both eyes. When I heard all that, I was worried, and as I was leaving the hospital, my spirit said, 'Go back and collect the X-rays and take them to church. Have you told God about it yet?' So I went back to the doctor and told him I wanted the X-rays. He first refused, asking me what I wanted to do with it. I told him I wanted to come back to Nigeria with it. Meanwhile, I knew what I wanted to do with it.

Immediately I got back to Nigeria, I came to church with the X-rays. At the time, I was new, and my faith was not that strong. However, I brought the X-rays with the intention that if only the Bishop could pray for me, touching the X-rays, I would be healed. I had that faith! I wanted to see the Bishop, so I waited the whole day. At about 3 p.m., he came downstairs, and I sat down, watching him as he talked with the pastors. While I gathered that he was on his way out on a trip, I wondered how to get across to him, especially as he did not know me. I looked at him and did not know what to do, wondering if he would leave without touching the X-rays. A few minutes later, the Bishop went outside, got into his car and left.

Ten minutes after he left, I entered the sanctuary and

went to the altar. I laid the X-rays there and said to God, 'Lord, this is what I intended to do, but I could not do it. Now, over to You'. I stayed there long enough to say all I wanted to say, and then I went home, feeling it was done.

Meanwhile, the doctor told me that if the operation was not carried out, all my tubes, including my respiratory tubes and outlets, would be blocked, and my face would be blown up. Lo and behold, since February 1996, my face has not blown up yet! It's been a year now, there is no blood in my brain, and I am still using my brain; I can see, read and do the things I could not do before! All the pains and aches I used to feel are gone. The two things they said would happen have not happened. I am sound and in good health! God has healed me. I return all the glory to God! ***— H. H.***

Let us see what more there is to Zion.

...Unto the heavenly Jerusalem...

Zion is described as a heavenly Jerusalem. This helps you understand why He says we are seated together with Him in heavenly places because Zion is where your heavenly status is made real.

...And to spirits of just men made perfect...

When you come to Zion, you enter into the midst of heavenly beings such as Elijah, Elisha, Gideon, Joshua, Paul, etc., and the anointing upon them rubs off on you. Remember that when king Saul came among the prophets, he prophesied, although it was not his lot. That tells you that your environment plays a vital role in your destiny.

> ***...To the general assembly and church of the first born...***

Zion is the Church of the Firstborn, where the spirits of just men gather. It is the general assembly of all those who have died and gone to heaven and we who are here on earth. When you understand this mystery, you will always have unique encounters every time you appear in church.

> ***And to Jesus the mediator of the new covenant and to the blood of sprinkling that speaks better things than the blood of Abel.***

There is always a sprinkling going on in the spiritual realm in Zion, and the Blood sprinkled is always speaking "Passover." Thus, whenever you come to meet with God, you renew your Passover insurance.

The reason we don't get the most out of Zion is that we don't know what it offers us. But Zion is a mysterious gathering, affording you all you need to do signs.

The Benefits of Zion

It Is The Place Of Cleansing

> ***But upon mount Zion shall be deliverance, and there shall be holiness; and the house of Jacob shall***

possess their possessions.

Obadiah 1:17

One thing that happens in Zion is constant cleansing. When sin is trying to catch up with you, and you come to church, somehow, perhaps through the choir ministration, when the offering is being taken or the teaching of the Word, the forces at work in Zion knock it out of you. Zion does not allow sin to stick to you.

Some time ago, someone wrote me a letter, and according to her, she was in the service one day and heard me say, "You proud wife; before your husband says one word, you have said ten." Immediately she said to herself, "That must be me he is talking about. But how did this man know my thoughts." While pondering on that word, she heard me say, "Get back home today, apologise to your husband and see if you will not see God in your home." So she got back home, apologised to her husband and a glorious new home was born!

Many proud hearts are undoing their destiny, and because they don't give heed to the Word in Zion, they remain that way. God wants to save you, so He has brought you to Zion. However, many people prefer to do some funny things at home or visit people and places rather than to be in church. Zion provides a place of cleansing that makes you a worthy vessel for signs and wonders.

That woman is now having a wonderful time in her

marriage because of the light she caught in Zion. She must have known that pride was bad and probably concluded she was not the only proud person. But that day, God caught up with her, and her home was preserved. Fellowship establishes your heritage in God. In Zion, you experience deliverances from the traps of the enemy and your possession is delivered to you.

The Place of Illumination

> ***Until I went into the sanctuary of God; then understood I their end.***
>
> *Psalm 73:17*

There is a strange light in Zion, a strange order of illumination, which comes from the light that emits from the altar at Zion. Zion is also the city of God, and according to 1 Timothy 6:16, God dwells in the light, and no unregenerated man can approach unto. The illumination at Zion is a result of the intensity of light that God dwells in.

Therefore, when the redeemed enters into God's presence, several things that he may have read at home, which he did not understand, become clear to him. Understanding comes as those mysteries are unfolded.

In these last days, Zion-addicted saints will do amazing signs in their generation because of the depths of insight they encounter in Zion. The knowledge they are receiving from Zion will result in a strange order of manifestation. You will see men and women picking up secrets from testimonies and having multiplied results using them.

> ***...But the people that do know their God shall be strong, and do exploits.***
>
> *Daniel 11:32*

By this same illumination, the Church will be absolutely in charge of the affairs of life because knowledge is a catalyst for the release of the anointing.

> ***So mightily grew the word of God and prevailed.***
>
> *Acts 19:20*

The Word of God grew so mightily in their midst that it prevailed, causing an eruption of signs and wonders, so much so that handkerchiefs and aprons taken from Paul were used to cast out devils. Friend, Zion is no ordinary place; it is the centre of illumination. It is where you encounter light that causes your understanding to blossom, bringing about signs!

Growth in the Word is enhanced in Zion. As you grow in the Word, you also grow in faith, which comes by the repeated hearing of the Word of God. Once faith comes, signs are bound to follow.

A Place of Growth

> ***The righteous shall flourish like the palm tree: he shall grow like a cedar in Lebanon.***

Those that be planted in the house of the Lord shall flourish in the courts of our God.

They shall still bring forth fruit in old age; they shall be fat and flourishing;

Psalm 92:12-14

Zion is the most fruitful hill on planet earth. Everything planted there blossoms without effort. Nobody needs to cry to possess his possessions because, at Zion, you naturally possess what is yours by heritage. Once you become a fellowship addict, you become a mysteriously flourishing saint. Things around you just keep flourishing.

We had one little tree on our pavement in Kaduna. The concrete had to be reinforced several times because the roots of the tree kept breaking through it. As I looked at the tree, I remembered what the Psalmist wrote and concluded that that was the mystery of Psalm 92 at work.

Friend, nothing can stop your flourishing when you are planted in Zion, not even if it is as strongly opposed to you as that concrete floor was to the little tree. When you are in genuine fellowship with God, you naturally blossom.

Some people do not flourish beyond certain degrees because they have made themselves overseers in the house of God instead of being participants. They see what everybody is doing wrong while they do just what they like. Remember, Zion is our Father's house, and Jesus is in charge, not you, so be careful! If you take your place in Zion, you will flourish naturally.

> ***Glorious things are spoken of thee, O city of God.***
>
> ***And of Zion it shall be said, This and that man was born in her: and the highest himself shall establish her.***
>
> ***The Lord shall count, when he writeth up the people, that this man was born there.***
>
> ***As well the singers as the players on instruments shall be there: all my springs are in thee.***
>
> *Psalm 87:3,5-7*

The time has come when the greatest honour will be to be named a citizen of Jerusalem. All our springs will be in Zion, meaning that the signs of a generation will be born there. Most of the outstanding inventions in science were by fellowship-addicted men. Men like James Clerk Maxwell, a great scientist in his time, who was described as having a very fertile mind.

No "Sunday Sunday" Christian (one who worships God only on Sundays) goes far in this race because the "servicing" he requires to keep his system in good shape and enhance his manifestations needs to be done regularly.

The Place of Servicing

No matter how expensive your car is, it regularly requires something to function effectively. That thing is called servicing. Except a car is serviced regularly, it won't serve you for long. God's servicing workshop for the saint is the Church, Zion. It is where all the connections to your spiritual manifestations are fine-tuned. Zion is where you grow in the areas that enhance your manifestation.

For instance, the Bible says, *Faith cometh by hearing, and hearing by the Word of God.* (Romans 10:17) In the growth connection, we learnt that at salvation, each one has a measure of faith, and what is done with that measure ultimately determines the extent of his manifestation.

There is a voice that sounds in Zion, coming straight at you from Heaven. As that voice sounds, and you catch it, you keep upgrading your knowledge of God, bringing you to greater levels of faith, and subsequently, you experience the manifestations of signs and wonders in your Christian walk.

That voice comes through apostles, prophets, evangelists, pastors and teachers to work on you until you come out a perfect man. Therefore, it is clear that God wants us to walk in the fullness of the stature of Christ (Ephesians 4:13), and He has designed Zion as the development centre.

So many barren women have become joyful mothers of children just by applying the things taught in Zion. All manner of ailments has been healed, and the dead raised as sons and daughters of Zion caught certain words and did exploits with them.

It is impossible to make it in life without responding positively to the demands of God. The farther you are from Zion, the farther you are from signs and wonders. However, when you get addicted to Zion, someday you will explode in signs and wonders like Philip and Stephen.

Watch those who don't service their cars regularly; they are the ones whose cars always need to be pushed in the rainy season, and the boys that help push their car charge them highly and sometimes insult them. The spiritual parallel of this is obvious: you cannot afford to miss service, or else you are giving the devil license to deal with you. Service is God's means of keeping your spiritual system functioning to build you up to a point where you explode in signs and wonders.

From today, I see you explode in the realms of miracles, signs and wonders. Whatever has been keeping you out of Zion wants to destroy your destiny, but I see a new love for Zion implanted in your heart, and I see you possess all your possessions!

Chapter Fifteen

Safeguarding The Miraculous

We have examined 12 connections that can help you command the supernatural. But as powerful as each of these connections are, there is what to do and what to avoid to stay on the wavelength of the miraculous. Just as once saved is not always saved, you need to maintain your walk in the miraculous. Here are some safeguards.

Watch The Company You Keep

> ***Be not deceived: evil communications corrupt good manners.***
>
> *1 Corinthians 15:33*

Wrong company disconnects you from realms of the miraculous. You cannot keep ungodly friends and expect to have godly manifestations; that would amount to making a mockery of God, and God cannot be mocked. You must be cautious in your choice of friends.

He that walketh with wise men shall be wise: but a companion of fools shall be destroyed.

Proverbs 13:20

Once you keep company with anti-miracle people, they will destroy your faith in the miraculous. They do not see things the way you do, so if you keep walking with them, you will soon be blinded to what you claim to see now.

Blessed is the man that walketh not in the counsel of the ungodly, nor standeth in the way of sinners, nor sitteth in the seat of the scornful.

But his delight is in the law of the Lord; and in his law doth he meditate day and night.

And he shall be like a tree planted by the rivers of water, that bringeth forth his fruit in his season; his leaf also shall not wither; and whatsoever he doeth shall prosper.

Psalm 1:1-3

If you want to live as a sign and maintain the flow of the miraculous, you must be careful where you stand, with whom you walk and whose counsel you operate with. You can't walk with the wrong people and have the right answers.

Paul, a man of great encounters, said evil communications corrupt good manners. There are people you walk with today that, except you part ways with them, your walk with God will never be prosperous.

Many years ago, I had a very close friend that never appreciated my commission. One day, he began to tear down the ministry God gave me in his preaching. That was the last day we had anything to do together. We had been so close that when my wife was to have our first son, he was the one who took her to the clinic. However, because I am conscious that only those who walk with the wise are wise, I cut off from him.

Friendship is not by force but by choice.

Can two walk together, except they be agreed?

Amos 3:3

Walking with someone you do not agree with is unwise. You are praying, he is mocking you; when you are studying the Word, he is laughing at you; when you love your wife, he mocks you for it! That kind of friendship will be to your destruction. Don't sell your birthright to the wrong company.

The Bible says in Isaiah 6:1 that it was in the year that king Uzziah died that Isaiah saw the Lord. Some of the friends you keep represent king Uzziah in your life. If you don't disconnect from them, you can never "see" God. You should not be somebody's friend just because you like his face. No, friendship means much more than that.

I have had to walk certain people trying to pollute my spirit out of my house. After all, the house is mine! Certain pastors will never preach in our church, no matter how anointed they are, because their character is suspect.

Some people have not experienced the purity God demands because they have refused to separate themselves from the corrupt company they keep.

> ***Wherefore come out from among them, and be ye separate, saith the Lord, and touch not the unclean thing; and I will receive you,***
>
> *2 Corinthians 6:17*

God instructs you to come out from among them, or He will reject you. And if God rejects you, those friends will not accept you. That was the experience of the prodigal son. Where were his friends when all his money was exhausted? They must have given him the wrong address, so he could not locate them again. After the devil stripped Adam and Eve naked, he went his way.

Some people you call your friends are enemies of your destiny, so cut off from them immediately.

> ***And being let go, they went to their own company, and reported all that the chief priests and elders had said unto them.***
>
> *Acts 4:23*

The disciples always returned to their company, so you too must have your own company — a group of people that see things the way you see them and believe in what you believe in; people who look forward to the same things you do. Find out if he loves the Lord as you do. Is he interested in the expansion of the kingdom? Does he do what the Word of God says? If you find such a person, he/she will motivate you to walk in the miraculous.

A young man shared his testimony in church one day. According to him, the previous day, a friend had come to his house and said, "There is nothing in this anointing oil thing." The things he heard dampened his faith. Little did he know that the attack on the anointing oil was a plan of the devil to cause problems in the near future. While in the classroom the following day, a lady fell down and stretched out. Everybody in the class fled, but this brother rushed to her side and prayed for her.

After praying for some time and there was no response from the lady, he went for his bottle of anointing oil. He forced her mouth open and poured some in. Shortly after, the lady was revived! If he had spent a few more days with that so-called friend, he would have lost complete confidence in the ability of God to heal through the anointing oil.

Be Sensitive

> ***After this there was a feast of the Jews; and Jesus went up to Jerusalem.***
>
> ***Now there is at Jerusalem by the sheep market***

a pool, which is called in the Hebrew tongue Bethesda, having five porches.

In these lay a great multitude of impotent folk, of blind, halt, withered, waiting for the moving of the water.

For an angel went down at a certain season into the pool, and troubled the water: whosoever then first after the troubling of the water stepped in was made whole of whatsoever disease he had.

And a certain man was there, which had an infirmity thirty and eight years.

John 5:1-5

The emphasis here is not on whosoever stepped in but who stepped in first. Those who stepped in were sensitive enough to see the angel just as he stepped into the water. Maybe they sat by the pool, with their fingers inside the water and plunged in to collect their miracles as soon as they saw the angel arrive. Some others had been there for years but sat under a tree somewhere, waiting for who would help them.

The fact that there was healing virtue in that pool is undeniable. People were coming and going away healed, but that man remained there permanently because he lacked the required sensitivity to encounter signs.

Every time God's Word is going on (either being preached or read in a book), the miracle pool is being troubled and sensitive people step in and collect their miracles. Men of action are men of manifestations. When you move at the instance of any revelation, you never lack manifestation. You don't need anyone to help you. All you need is, "God said it, I believe it and that settles it!"

When I was a victim of tuberculosis, I had a very severe attack one night at about 1:30 a.m. I came out of my room, stood on a rock and said, "Jesus Christ, if it is true that You did all the miracles written in Matthew, Mark, Luke and John, then I have had enough of this thing." And that was the end of it.

I was responding to the truth I had drunk in from the gospel. I stood up that same day and took delivery of my miracle. Only smart people are go-getters. It takes spiritual smartness to maintain the flow of signs.

> ***I sleep, but my heart waketh: it is the voice of my beloved that knocketh, saying, Open to me, my sister, my love, my dove, my undefiled: for my head is filled with dew, and my locks with the drops of the night.***
>
> ***I have put off my coat; how shall I put it on? I have washed my feet; how shall I defile them?***
>
> ***My beloved put in his hand by the hole of the door, and my bowels were moved for him.***
>
> ***I rose up to open to my beloved; and my hands dropped with myrrh, and my fingers with sweet smelling myrrh, upon the handles of the lock.***

I opened to my beloved; but my beloved had withdrawn himself, and was gone: my soul failed when he spake: I sought him, but I could not find him; I called him, but he gave me no answer.

The watchmen that went about the city found me, they smote me, they wounded me; the keepers of the walls took away my veil from me.

I charge you, O daughters of Jerusalem, if ye find my beloved, that ye tell him, that I am sick of love.

Song Of Solomon 5:2-8

This emphasises the importance of quick response, sensitivity and spiritual vigilance in maintaining the flow of signs in your life. Every time a word strikes in your heart, stand up and act on it immediately. The Bible says in Revelations 3:20 that God stands at the door of your heart, knocking with insight from His Word. If you delay, you may be denied, so strike when the iron is hot!

Remember the testimony of the man that suffered from typhoid fever for nine years? He discovered what to do from reading the book, *The Healing Balm*. But he wanted to postpone taking action, suddenly a voice came to him, saying, "Do it now!" He then cursed typhoid fever with his legs crossed, and according to him, something dropped off him immediately!

Friend, the Holy Ghost operates mostly on sudden frequencies. On the day of Pentecost, He came suddenly.

In the house of Cornelius, He also came suddenly upon the Gentiles. If His manifestations are on sudden frequencies, it takes highly sensitive men to cash in on them.

We have lost too many things to insensitivity. If we know what God is saying per time and cash in on it, we will keep on commanding signs and wonders. God is always on the move; if you are not sensitive, you will miss what He is set to do.

It is time to put a motion to the revelation you have received; so you will have a revolution. Those things that have struck you as you read this book are the things that if you hold fast to and operate by, heaven will place a seal of approval on them. Your explanations irritate God. You are a son of manifestation; everything is supposed to respond to you. You are created to make things work; stop making excuses!

Do you really want signs and wonders to follow you? Then be sensitive to the move of the Spirit. Remember what happened in Acts 3. Peter was sensitive enough to know that was the lame man's day for a miracle.

There is a great day ahead for you, but you require spiritual sensitivity to walk into it. Stop looking for pity; the world is waiting for your manifestations. Get angry at those negative situations around you, you are up to it now. Stop waiting for miracles; if you wait; you will waste. Now is your time!

Don't Give Room To Fear

Fear is not a psychological state but a trap of the enemy. Fear is a spirit (2 Timothy 1:7). It is the complete opposite of the Spirit of boldness and faith. It brings men into captivity.

When Satan was looking for a way to afflict Job, he introduced fear into his heart. The moment he gave in to fear, he lost his victory (Job 3:25).

Spiritual blindness is a major reason for the fears that come upon us and take us captive.

Elisha's servant in 2 Kings 6 was afraid because he saw the horses and chariots that were out against them. But Elisha was relaxed because he saw better. When his servant's eyes were opened, he saw the mountains filled with horses and chariots of fire! So don't give in to fear; it can rob you of signs and wonders.

Have A Miracle Mind

> ***For as he thinketh in his heart, so is he...***
>
> *Proverbs 23:7*

It takes miracle thoughts to command and maintain the flow of signs. You can't think of obstacles and have miracles. You can't think of impossibilities and expect possibilities. Often, many people allow thoughts of impossibilities becloud their minds. They ask, "How can this be? You see, I want to be very practical. After all, we live in a world of realities, so we have to deal with facts. Now tell me, how do you think I can build a house under these harsh economic circumstances?"

That man carries obstacle thoughts, yet he is looking for miracles. The two don't go together. Look at Abraham, the Bible says concerning him:

> ***And being not weak in faith, he considered not his own body now dead, when he was about an hundred years old, neither yet the deadness of Sarah's womb:***
>
> ***He staggered not at the promise of God through unbelief; but was strong in faith, giving glory to God;***
>
> ***And being fully persuaded that, what he had promised, he was able also to perform.***
>
> *Romans 4:19-21*

His age had no place in his mind. Although he and Sarah had passed childbearing age, his mind was closed to all negative factors. He refused to consider those things that could cause him to stagger. Instead, he chose to consider the ability of God, His omnipotence. Abraham judged God faithful, so he became the "Father of Faith."

His confidence in God made him persuaded that what God had promised, He was also able to perform. Abraham believed that whatever God said was good enough for him.

No one can maintain the flow of miracles without a miracle mind. The woman with the issue of blood had this miracle mind I am talking about, and that turned her captivity. She thought her way through to her miracle.

In 2 Kings 5, the Bible talks about a great Syrian general called Naaman. He was a leper, and his greatest problem was not leprosy but negative thoughts. He was a victim of negative thoughts. In verse 6, the king of Syria sent a letter to the king of Israel, saying, "Now when this letter is come unto thee, behold, I have therewith sent Naaman my servant to thee, that thou mayest recover him of his leprosy."

He got to Elisha the prophet, who, without coming out to see him, instructed him to go and dip himself seven times in the river Jordan and be cleansed. But instead of being excited, he was offended.

> ***But Naaman was wroth, and went away, and said, Behold, I thought, He will surely come out to me, and stand, and call on the name of the Lord his God, and strike his hand over the place, and recover the leper.***
>
> *2 Kings 5:11*

Just like Naaman, many are in trouble, yet, they are offended by the truth. The enemy has polluted their minds in order to punish them. It was against his destiny until his servants said:

...My father, if the prophet had bid thee do some great thing, wouldest thou not have done it? how much rather then, when he saith to thee, Wash, and be clean?

Then went he down, and dipped himself seven times in Jordan, according to the saying of the man of God: and his flesh came again like unto the flesh of a little child, and he was clean.

2 Kings 5:13-14

His thoughts stood in the way of his miracle. Thoughts are so powerful that they either make you or break you, but they never leave you neutral. Here is the story of another man:

Then Elisha said, Hear ye the word of the Lord; Thus saith the Lord, To morrow about this time shall a measure of fine flour be sold for a shekel, and two measures of barley for a shekel, in the gate of Samaria.

Then a lord on whose hand the king leaned answered the man of God, and said, Behold, if the Lord would make windows in heaven, might this thing be? And he said, Behold, thou shalt see it with thine eyes, but shalt not eat thereof.

2 Kings 7:1-2

His thoughts hindered him from partaking of the miraculous. Perhaps he thought within himself, "I am in charge of the food supply in this country. I can't be deceived by this 'bush' prophet." He lost out of partaking in the miraculous because nobody thinks impossibility thoughts and experiences possibilities. No one thinks obstacles and has miracles!

After we had our first son, the doctor said he had jaundice. But I said, "He does not have jaundice." The doctor replied, "You mean I don't know my job?" I insisted, "My son cannot have jaundice!" And the matter ended there. It will interest you to know that I was too busy to examine his eyes. That is a miracle mind.

Renew Your Mind

> ***And be not conformed to this world: but be ye transformed by the renewing of your mind, that ye may prove what is that good, and acceptable, and perfect, will of God.***
>
> *Romans 12:2*

Since no one commands the flow of miracles without a miracle mind, you need to renew your mind, or else you remain a victim of obstacles. Paul said:

> ***Let this mind be in you, which was also in Christ Jesus:***
>
> *Philippians 2:5*

All the mighty acts that Jesus did came by the operation of His mind. Remember how He fed the 5,000. It was written concerning Him, *And this he said to prove him: for he himself knew what he would do.*

Jesus had a fertile mind, so the miraculous attended to Him naturally.

It is impossible to operate the mind of Christ and the world not mind you.

Consider Jesus

> ***For consider him that endured such contradiction of sinners against himself, lest ye be wearied and faint in your minds.***
>
> *Hebrews 12:3*

You are always considering something at every point in time. The mind is never completely empty. Instead of considering the situations of life, it is time to consider the abilities of God. Anytime you are fainting in your mind, it is because you are considering the negative situations of your life.

Fainting in the mind leads to staggering in the legs. Abraham did not stagger because he was always considering God's ability to handle his case. That had him settled and prevented him from fainting and his legs from staggering.

Think On These Things

> ***Finally, brethren, whatsoever things are true, whatsoever things are honest, whatsoever things are just, whatsoever things are pure, whatsoever things are lovely, whatsoever things are of good***

report; if there be any virtue, and if there be any praise, think on these things.

Philippians 4:8

This is the New Testament thinking syllabus. It makes us understand there are certain things you must never think about and what you should think about. Let me ask you, "Do you want to walk in realms of the miraculous? Do you want miracle finances, miracle health, miracle jobs, a miracle home, a miracle business, miracle babies?" Then think about these things!

Every time your mind appears to be wandering off, call it to order! Don't conclude it is impossible to make it in Nigeria, or wherever you are. Those negative thoughts hinder you from making it here. God has great plans for you, and that is why He said:

Keep thy heart with all diligence; for out of it are the issues of life.

Proverbs 4:23

If the woman with the issue of blood spoke within herself and was healed, you must be careful what you say within yourself. If you are saying, "I cannot be sick" or "I cannot be poor," you are programming yourself to encounter miracle health and wealth.

The Canaanite woman in Matthew 15:21-28 had a miracle mind. She was too set for her miracle to be stopped. The apostles attempted to stop her could not.

At her importunity, Jesus said, *O woman, great is thy faith: be it unto thee even as thou wilt.*

No matter how hard you pray, until you think right, you cannot live right. Until you think great, you will never become great. Until you think miracle thoughts, you will never have miracles.

The Secret Of Rest

Rest is the evidence of faith, and nothing happens without faith. Anxiety is an expression of doubt and unbelief. The Bible says of the doubtful:

> ***For let not that man think that he shall receive any thing of the Lord.***
>
> *James 1:7*

The supernatural cannot manifest for the doubtful. Until you truly restful spiritually, mentally and psychologically on any issue of life, God cannot step in. We are living in a restless world. It is the jet set age where there is a lot of jostling and bustling about, and consciously or unconsciously, you find even believers caught up in this web. But what saith the scriptures?

> ***Except the LORD build the house, they labour in vain that build it.***
>
> *Psalm 127:1*

The battle is not to the strong, nor is the race to the swift; everything depends on the Lord's mercy, which is only enjoyed by those who are at rest in the Lord their God.

Rest is a sign of belief, and it attracts and compels the attention of the supernatural for intervention in any situation.

> ***For we which have believed do enter into rest...***
>
> *Hebrews 4:3*

There is a rest that every believer must enter into if he wants God to manifest in his situation. Until you enter into that rest, don't deceive yourself by claiming you believe. Your entering into rest is the only biblical evidence you have believed.

The Practice Of Rest

Rest implies that you have ceased doing it yourself; you have ceased from your own efforts. This is a divine principle in fighting battles. You must cease from fruitless labour and rest in the Lord, for He only fights for those who hold their peace and wait upon Him in confidence. God's saving hand can only be stretched in the direction of those who stand still.

> ***The LORD shall fight for you, and ye shall hold your peace.***
>
> *Exodus 14:14*

Also, in Psalm 46:10, the Word of God says:

> ***Be still, and know that I am God...***

God never fights until you are in a position of complete rest in Him. Hannah had been barren for many years; she wanted a child, and the taunting provocations of her mate almost drove her out of her mind. She worried and complained. She blamed God, her husband and her rival. In fact, she blamed everybody. Was God blind to her pathetic situation? Did He not love her? Could He not help her? These were the questions that kept on coming up from the depth of her being. But the mighty hand of God could not move on her behalf as long as she was restless.

Some people think that their much worrying and crying will move God. This is another lie from the pit of hell. God is not moved by tears of anxiety, which are always accusative in nature. He is moved only by His Word. Hannah was ignorant of this, so she fretted, wept and could not eat.

Then God's mercy prevailed. Instead of complaining, she was impressed upon to table the matter before God. She was still weeping, but, this time, with a difference. She poured out her soul to God as she prayed and made a vow to put a stamp to her seriousness. By so doing, she handed her situation over to God and left it with Him. The **Bible** says:

> ***...So the woman went her way, and did eat, and her countenance was no more sad.***
>
> *1 Samuel 1:18*

She stepped out of the situation, and she found rest. It took her stepping out for God to step in. She handed over the battle to God, and He took over. Then the supernatural manifested, and she had a baby boy.

In the wrestling doubles matches, your partner can only step in after you have tapped his hand and stepped out of the ring. Stepping into the ring while your partner is still inside is regarded as foul play. When confronted with any situation, touch God's hand in prayer and step out for Him to step in. The act of stepping out is the act of rest. A problem that drives sleep from your eyes is not one for which God's mighty hand will move. The mouth of the Lord has spoken:

> ***For thus saith the Lord GOD, the Holy One of Israel; In returning and rest shall ye be saved; in quietness and in confidence shall be your strength...***
>
> *Isaiah 30:15*

Your salvation lies in your resting in the Lord. Salvation implies deliverance, healing, prosperity, etc. God has not called you to meditate on your problems. He has called you to meditate on His Word; this is what brings rest. If you claim to trust God, you must have rest in your spirit, soul and body. Maintain quietness. Sit or stand still.

There was never a strain in Jesus during His earthly ministry; He was always composed. He was in the same boat as His disciples, but while the disciples were running here and there, trying desperately to save themselves, He was at peace. I don't believe Jesus was actually sleeping. He saw His disciples struggling. He saw them fretting and worrying; He saw the wind and the storm; He saw the boat getting full to overflowing with water, but He was not moved. He was at rest.

When they remembered Him and called Him into the situation, He spoke, and the supernatural manifested. The wind obeyed; the storm ceased. I discovered that my greatest crusades and meetings were those held when I had to get one-hour sleep just before the programme. Rest is an absolute necessity.

Do you not know that the time God speaks best to His servants and seekers is in the cool of the day? Why so? The hours that make the cool of the day are those hours when there is quiet and rest everywhere; then He speaks, and He always speaks in a still small voice. A "still small voice" can't be heard in the midst of turmoil. Practice resting in Him and watch what happens to those seemingly great and impossible situations confronting you.

If only you will rest in the Lord after making your requests known to Him, the storms of life will bow down to you. Let God take over the situation for you and stand still and see the salvation of the Lord manifested through the release of the supernatural in you.

It Is Your Turn!

And now, brethren, I commend you to God, and to the word of his grace, which is able to build you up, and to give you an inheritance among all them which are sanctified.

Acts 20:32

The miraculous is yours for the taking, but it shall not be by wishes. If you have been wishing you can work miracles, stop wishing and start working! Nothing works until you work it. The Bible does not talk about the gift of waiting for miracles but of the working of miracles. So, don't wait for miracles; go and work them!

Just like the man at the pool of Bethesda, who waited for 38 years, those who wait end up wasting. If Jesus had not come to his rescue, he would have died beside the miracle pool. What an irony!

Should you be childless now, don't say, "I know someday I will be pregnant!" This is the day, and now is the time! Your miracle is available today, so why are you wasting and waiting until tomorrow?

If the woman with the issue of blood, despite her

weakness, could press her way to her miracle, then it is your press that will hand over your prize to you. Perhaps you have been waiting for Jesus to come to you. In case He hasn't come, you go to Him! You cannot afford to be like the man at the pool of Bethesda, who was so unprepared for a miracle. Friend, you can go to Jesus today for attention!

Let me reiterate that you are created for signs, not for sighs; you are created to be envied, not to be pitied. You are created for glory, not for shame; for beauty, not for ashes; for dignity, not for ignominy. However, your position is not decided by God but by your dedication to the end-time programme of God.

We have had the Acts of the Apostles; now, it is time for the Acts of the Church. It won't just be by the pastors and apostles but by every member of the Body of Christ, taking their positions in the move of God. This is where you belong!

The time has come when you will stand in your shop or office as a sign. That means your business will respond to your status as a sign, and everything will bow to your authority.

We must not gather around to pray "If it be thy will..." prayers anymore. His will is you in action! That is His will for mankind. You cannot afford to sit around in the church as a prayer project. It is time to get up on your feet and take your place in God!

I release you into a world of signs and wonders!

I release you into the miraculous realm of life!

Because you believe, signs will follow you from now on!

From today, you shall no longer live with obstacles!

Everywhere you turn, the signs of heaven will answer to you!

Go forth and make it happen!

ABOUT THE *Author*

David O. Oyedepo, called to be an Apostle with a mandate to liberate the world through the preaching of the Word of Faith, has for nearly four decades been part of the ongoing charismatic revival sweeping across the African continent today. His faith-based teachings have literarily transformed millions of lives around the world.

He is the Founder and President of the Living Faith Church Worldwide also known as Winners' Chapel International, with a network of thousands of Churches in Nigeria and several other nations across the continents of the world.

Till date, he has published over 90 impactful titles most of which have been translated to major languages of the world such as French, Chinese, Spanish etc. with over twenty million copies in circulation.

He is the Senior Pastor of the Faith Tabernacle, Canaanland, Ota, Nigeria, with a 50,000-seat sanctuary, reputed to be the largest church facility in the world. The church currently runs five services on Sunday morning with over 300,000 worshippers, making her one of the largest church congregations in the world.

His mission has established educational institutions across all levels in Nigeria, with Covenant and Landmark Universities taking large strides towards becoming world class universities.

He is married to Faith and they are blessed with sons, daughters and grandchildren.

Books By Dr David Oyedepo

- Wonders of Kingdom Stewardship
- Following The Path Of The Eagle
- The Exceeding Riches Of His Grace
- Not By Power Nor By Might
- The Turnaround Power Of The Word
- Understanding The Power Of Faith
- The Breakthrough Power Of Vision
- On Eagle's Wings
- The Unlimited Power Of Faith
- In Pursuit Of Vision
- Pillars Of Destiny
- Signs & Wonders Today
- Exploits In Ministry
- Winning The War Against Poverty
- Walking In Dominion
- Possessing Your Possession
- The Wisdom That Works
- Exploits Of Faith
- Anointing For Exploits
- Understanding The Power Of Praise
- Walking In Newness Of Life
- Maximise Destiny
- Commanding The Supernatural
- Winning Invisible Battles
- Success Systems
- Understanding Financial Prosperity
- Success Strategies
- Understanding Your Covenant Right
- Miracle Meal
- Exploring the Riches of Redemption
- Anointing For Breakthrough
- Excellency Of Wisdom
- Breaking Financial Hardship
- The Release Of Power
- Walking In The Miraculous

Books By Dr David Oyedepo

- Satan Get Lost!
- The Winning Wisdom
- Walking In Wisdom
- The Healing Balm
- Manifestations Of The Spirit
- Breaking The Curses Of Life
- Overcoming Forces Of Wickedness
- You Shall Not Be Barren!
- Exploring The Secrets Of Success
- Winning Prayer
- Understanding The Anointing
- Fulfilling Your Days
- Towards Mental Exploits
- Understanding Vision
- Understanding Divine Direction
- The Force Of Freedom
- Born To Win
- The Shower Of Blessing
- Riding On Prophetic Wings
- All You Need To Have All Your needs Met
- Operating In The Supernatural
- Ruling Your World
- Success in Marriage *(Co-authored with Faith Oyedepo)*
- The Blood Triumph
- Keys To Divine Health
- Winning Faith
- Conquering Controlling Powers
- Put Your Angels To Work
- Covenant Wealth
- Keys To Answered Prayer
- Miracle Seed
- The Hidden Covenant Of Blessing

INSIDE VIEW OF Faith Tabernacle

Dr David Oyedepo is the Founding President of the Living Faith Church Worldwide Inc. and the Senior Pastor of the Faith Tabernacle, a 50,000 capacity sanctuary located in Canaanland, Ota, a suburb of Lagos, Nigeria.

The construction of this gigantic architectural masterpiece was completed within twelve months and dedicated on September 18, 1999, built totally debt-free and without any foreign inputs! To God alone be all the glory.

Today, Faith Tabernacle stands as the home of signs and wonders for men and women all over the world, who keep coming in droves to worship the King of kings and the Lord of lords, Jesus Christ the Son of the Living God.

OUTSIDE VIEW OF FAITH TABERNACLE

OVERVIEW OF FAITH TABERNACLE

Visit our website for more information: www.faithtabernacle.org.ng